The Hanging Pit

The Haunting of Bodmin Jail

also by Richard Estep

In Search of the Paranormal
Haunted Longmont
The World's Most Haunted Hospitals
The Farnsworth House Haunting
Trail of Terror
Colorado UFOs
The Devil's Coming to Get Me
The Fairfield Haunting
Haunted Healthcare
The Horrors of Fox Hollow Farm
Building the Write Life

As co-author

The Haunting of Asylum 49
Spirits of the Cage
The Black Monk of Pontefract

The Hanging Pit

The Haunting of Bodmin Jail

Richard Estep

To Spencer,

May your courage and determination inspire others to become empowered with the desire to find their true identity. Your bravery is a testament to your willingness to succeed.

Love, Dad. (Wes)

Contents

Foreword
Introduction
1. Three Sundays
2. "Good Luck – You're Going to Need it…"
3. Haunted History
4. Apparition in the Cellar
5. "You Don't Really Know Him."
6. Fed by the Faeries
7. Warders
8. "My God, You've Just Changed…"
9. The Naval Prison
10. The Hanging Pit
11. Glassed
12. Round Two
13. "It's Not a 'Who.' It's a 'What.'"
14. Aggressive
15. "You'll be Back."
16. Boom
Acknowledgments

Foreword

I was first introduced to the author about two years ago after I had read his book *The Worlds Most Haunted Hospitals,* and reached out to him, thinking he would make a good guest on my podcast, *Haunted Histories.* I was not to be disappointed.

It was after that initial conversation that we became what I would like to think of as firm friends, and many furthur collaborations together have ensued. It was only recently that he told me that all this time I had been pronouncing his surname wrong…I was mortified, but he thought it was absolutely hilarious, and that is the Richard Estep that some do not realize when they read his books.

He has a somewhat dry sense of humor, but one which comes through in droves, especially when you're locked into a location for 10 or 12 hours with him. This ability to have a laugh is incredibly important when you are investigating a place as devoid of frivolity and gregariousness as Bodmin Jail. It is very hard not to empathize with the poor souls who were imprisoned there for offences as trivial as stealing a loaf of bread. When you look back through the list of executions attributed to Bodmin – although it must be stressed that most of them took place outside of the prison grounds – whilst murder may be deemed an acceptable crime to receive the death penalty, it's hard to justify things such as forgery, arson (setting fire, in this instance, to a corn stack!) and even stealing a sheep as being hangable offences, but they were. I wonder if it is this sense of dread and fear that pervades the prison that makes it such an attractive place for historians and paranormal enthusiasts to visit.

I am no stranger to the prison myself. You will see my name mentioned in Richard's book on the jail, as I was lucky enough to join him on phase two of his investigations in researching this tome, which I was beyond excited about. The love that Richard and his wife Laura have for the county of Cornwall is very evident in the way they both talk about it, the kind of positiveness which is always refreshing and revitalizing to see and hear. This invitation was in part due to the fact that I had been privy to a few experiences of my own when visiting the now tourist attraction back in 2014, which you will be able to read more about later on.

There are many theories as to why Bodmin Jail is so active – and it is! – and in listening to people such as Kirsten Honey, who is the resident paranormal liaison for the prison, you can see how it draws people to it like a magnet. Is this because of the limestone rock on which it lays? Is it due to the water which passes by, or is it purely due to the amount of intense energy that has seeped into its very foundations over these years, no one would really know? What I would say, however, is get yourself a drink, turn off the television and let Richard take you on a journey into this eerie but also beautiful old piece of Cornish history.

Penny Griffiths-Morgan

Introduction

"We who live in prison, and in who's lives there is no event but sorrow, have to measure time by throbs of pain, and the record of bitter moments." —Oscar Wilde

It was while writing *The World's Most Haunted Hospitals* that I first noticed a rather curious thing. The book, which looked at reports of paranormal activity in medical facilities both past and present, was an opportunity for me to examine places in which human beings had endured a great deal of pain and suffering. As most paranormal investigators and armchair enthusiasts will tell you, where one finds strong emotion — whether positive or negative — one also tends to find ghosts.

While there was no shortage of ghost stories to be found when I spoke to a host of doctors, nurses, and other medical staff, perhaps the darkest and most disturbing stories came from the lunatic asylums, where the inmates (considering the sheer brutality that many of them suffered, it seems unfair to refer to them as 'patients') were incarcerated for months, years, and sometimes decades upon end.

That started me thinking about jails and prisons. During

my twenty-three-year career as a paranormal investigator, I had only investigated one such place, the jail in a small mountain town in my adopted state of Colorado, named Cripple Creek. It had been an extraordinary experience. Along with a number of fellow paranormal investigators, I was fortunate enough to experience disembodied voices, phantom footsteps, and perhaps strangest of all, a colleague saw my *doppleganger* standing on the upper cell block, while the actual me was sitting safe and sound in a cell, with a colleague standing guard in the doorway.

While prowling the hallways of the jail and spending some time in the cells, staring at the four walls and contemplating the steel bars that penned me in, I found it easy to put myself in the shoes of someone who was forcibly deprived of their freedom and locked away in such a place. In terms of the raw emotion that would be generated, whether one was innocent or guilty really didn't matter; either way, there would be plenty of time for the inmate to brood about what they had or hadn't done. Imagine the sheer amount of pent-up anger, resentment, and sometimes despair that would be generated over the time of the average prison sentence, multiply it by the number of prisoners incarcerated there, and you suddenly have a very potent energy source for paranormal activity.

Some have put forward the idea that such negative emotion can create a sort of "psychic scar," one that can perhaps be picked up at a future time by certain people, those who are suitably attuned to their surrounding environment. If that is indeed the case, it should come as no surprise to us that places of imprisonment often turn out to be haunted by the echoes of inmates (and often jailers) past.

The more I thought about it, the more I wanted to explore the idea further. Now, all that I needed was an abandoned prison, preferably one with a solid track record of being haunted. One of the first places that came to mind was Bodmin Jail in Cornwall, England, which had it all, and more besides: a rich and colorful history, a fearsome reputation, and a skilled team of in-house paranormal experts with whom I could consult and cooperate.

When I reached out to their representatives, the owners of Bodmin Jail were amenable to my visiting the place and carrying out an investigation of my own. I wanted to spend some time there looking for answers, trying to connect with the spirits of the jail and seeing if I could gather some evidence of their existence – or, on the other hand, debunk some of the stories that were circulating about the place.

Once permission was secured, I made arrangements to fly in from America in the early part of 2018, and brought in some fellow paranormal investigators to accompany me. My friends and colleagues Stephen and Lesley put in the lion's share of the work, while Gaynor and Caroline also joined us for part of the investigation.

It is an open secret amongst the community of paranormal enthusiasts that much of what we do in the field is often fruitless and relatively dull. There is a lot of sitting around monitoring equipment, setting up experiments, taking baseline readings, and waiting for something to happen. All too often, that 'something' never comes.

Fortunately for us, Bodmin Jail would prove to be the exception rather than the rule. The grand old place wasn't going to disappoint us in the slightest.

Let's go and find out why, shall we?

Richard Estep
Longmont, Colorado
June 6, 2020

CHAPTER ONE
Three Sundays

On July 20, 1909, the last execution to ever be carried out in Cornwall took place at Bodmin. The condemned man was one William Hampton, aged 24, who had been sentenced to death for the crime of murdering his girlfriend, Emily Barnes Trewarthen Tredea. The poor girl was just 16 years old at the time her life was so tragically cut short.

According to the prosecution, the motive was a simple one. Emily no longer wanted to see William. Rather than allow her to break off their relationship and leave him, he chose instead to strangle her to death.

Hanging a man (or, for that matter, a woman) was no simple matter. It required significantly more effort than just running a rope from a beam and fashioning a noose; indeed, a number of very precise calculations had to take place, factoring in such variables as the height and weight of the prisoner, in order to determine exactly how far their body needed to fall in order to ensure a quick and clean execution. This technique is known as 'the long drop,' and was devised by the famed executioner William Marwood, who plied his trade at Bodmin Jail, among other places. The method is still in use today — Iraqi dictator Saddam Hussein was one of the more recent recipients.

Do it right, and the condemned person's neck breaks quickly and cleanly, completely bisecting the spinal cord, in addition to fracturing the second cervical vertebrae just beneath the skull. Without an intact spinal cord, impulses from the central nervous system are unable to reach the muscles responsible for respiration, and the person 'dancing at the end of the rope' (as the expression goes) is no longer able to breathe. Respiratory arrest sets in almost immediately, and cardiac arrest follows right on its heels. The person hanging is rendered unconscious due to the lack of oxygenated blood reaching the brain, and therefore feels little, if any pain — or so it is believed.

When the job is done sloppily, a much uglier sequence of events can take place. If the executioner uses too much rope, the falling body gains too much speed, and when the rope suddenly jerks taut, there can sometimes be sufficient force to rip the condemned person's head from their body. The hanging has just become an accidental decapitation.

An unintentional beheading at least has the virtue of being quick. If the rope is too short, however, then the condemned doesn't fall as far as they need to in order to sustain a broken neck. Instead, the noose bites deeply into the neck and throat, effectively strangling the victim to death. Strangulation is a drawn-out and very unpleasant way to go — though in the case of William Hampton, who had strangled his young girlfriend, many might have seen it as a fitting punishment. There are eyewitness reports of botched hangings in which the hanged party kicked and struggled desperately, twisting to and fro at the end of the rope while the life was slowly choked out of them. The face and neck would swell up grotesquely as the pressure built inside the head. Eyes would bulge out of their sockets, and it wasn't unheard of for the condemned to void their bowels and bladder, one last indignity before death finally took them.

It could take anywhere between ten minutes to half an hour for somebody to die of strangulation, and professional executioners went to great pains to ensure that it did not happen on their watch. During public hangings, family members of the soon-to-be-deceased were sometimes seen to run out of the gathered crowd and tug on the legs of their dangling family member, helping to put a swift end to their misery.

William Hampton spent his 24th (and final) birthday at Bodmin Jail, and the last month of his life was spent in the specialized Condemned Cell. Once the sentence of death had been conferred by a judge, the law required that three consecutive Sundays be allowed to pass before the execution could be carried out. This allowed the condemned ample time to reflect upon their crime and to prepare themselves to meet their maker — or so the theory went. It is easy to imagine the gut-twisting tension that the guilty party must have felt as day after day passed, the sense of sick anticipation building as the day of the hanging drew near. They were kept under the watchful eye of two jail guards around the clock, day and night, to ensure that they didn't commit suicide and therefore evade the hangman's noose.

In the United States today, the process of appealing a death sentence is lengthy and interminable. It is not at all unusual for prisoners to spend decades on death row, many dying of old age and natural causes before their date with the electric chair or lethal injection. Things were very different back in William Hampton's day. His appeal was rejected within just a few days of sentencing.

On the day of the hanging, Hampton was taken from the jail to the hanging shed in a somber procession, escorted by a phalanx of guards and other members of the prison staff. The executioner, Mr. Pierrepoint, took great care to place him in precisely the right spot above the pit, then bound his legs together and looped the noose around his neck, making sure that the knot was properly positioned for maximum effect.

Once he was satisfied that all was ready, Pierrepoint operated the lever, opening up the trap door. Instantly, Hampton plunged some seven feet down into the hanging pit. The rope snapped taut with an audible crack, jerking the condemned man back and arresting his fall. As there is no written record of there being any complications, we can assume that the hangman's knot had done its job, sending William Hampton into respiratory arrest. Not long afterward, his heart stopped beating.

Once all signs of life had left it, William Hampton's body was then left to hang for an hour, before being taken down and carried away. A physician in attendance confirmed that he was in fact dead. Executed prisoners were not allowed to be buried in public cemeteries, and so his remains were interred within the grounds of Bodmin Jail in a simple grave, topped only with a floral tribute provided by his next of kin.

So went the final execution within the walls of Bodmin Jail. One hundred and ten years later, I would step up onto that very same platform myself, escorting a hooded prisoner by the arm and retracing the last footsteps of William Hampton and his entourage of escorts.

It was an experience that I will never forget.

CHAPTER TWO
"Good Luck – You're Going to Need it…"

Much like the rest of England, Cornwall in January tends to be cold and windy. The skies are slate-grey and almost perpetually overcast. During the five days we spend there in early 2018, it rarely stops raining. The weather ranges from light showers to torrential downpours, and everything in between. We even have flurries of snow one night, although they last for no more than fifteen minutes, after which the clouds part and allow patches of clear blue sky to peek through.

It's a long drive from London's Heathrow Airport to the county of Cornwall, and I make full use of the opportunity to do a little background reading on our destination. My first stop before investigating any British case is always with my favorite ghost hunter and author, the legendary Peter Underwood. In the event that you're unfamiliar with his work, I can highly recommend any of the numerous books that Mr. Underwood authored down through the years. As a young boy growing up in Leicestershire, I had devoured every single book of his that I could find in the local library, checking them out multiple times and reading each one from cover to cover, before starting all over again the next day. Many was the night I spent huddled under the blankets in my bedroom, reading one of the great investigator's books with the help of a flashlight.

A former president of the Ghost Club Society and a member of the Society for Psychical Research, Peter Underwood spent a long and distinguished career investigating supposedly-haunted locations across the length and breadth of the United Kingdom, and sometimes overseas as well. He seems to have had a fascination for Bodmin Jail, and wrote about it in several of his books, including *Ghosts of Cornwall* and *Peter Underwood's Guide to Ghosts and Haunted Places*.

According to his sources, numerous different types of paranormal phenomena have been documented at Bodmin Jail. These include the sound of keys rattling inside the old cell blocks and the ringing of phantom bells; the sound of a variety of footsteps stamping around the stone floors at all hours; nebulous ghostly figures being sighted; and a pervasive sense of despair which, Underwood said, was a consequence of the many executions that had taken place there over the years.

One piece of recorded phenomena is particularly

intriguing: claims that dogs refuse to go in certain parts of the building, which would come back into my mind later on when our taxi driver reported his own dog refusing to behave itself in the area of the condemned man's cell. In my view, this adds a little extra validation to Mr. Underwood's account.

Our home away from home is the infamous Jamaica Inn, which sits high up on a lonely and windswept stretch of the moor between the towns of Bodmin and Bolventor. The subject of a novel of the same name written by Dame Daphne Du Maurier, which was later adapted for film and directed by Alfred Hitchcock (and more recently, a much-maligned BBC mini-series of the same name) the inn was once frequented by smugglers and travelers in equal measure. Jamaica Inn has its own reputation for ghosts, and I have made sure to pick one of the most active rooms — Room 5, which is said to be haunted by the spirit of a young girl.

My good friend Stephen Weidner has accompanied me all the way from the United States. He and I have spent more than ten years conducting paranormal investigations together, in locations such as firehouses, prisons, and hospitals across my adopted state of Colorado and throughout the United States.

In addition to being a seasoned paranormal investigator, Stephen also happens to be a Catholic priest, belonging to the Sacred Order of St. Michael. Despite being an agnostic, I sometimes find it handy to bring along some spiritual 'heavy artillery' to an investigation, just in case it turns out to be a little darker in nature than it first appears. I learned this lesson the hard way when something negative seemed to attach itself to me after an investigation, beginning to manifest in various unpleasant ways around my home. When things finally came to a head, Stephen kindly offered to cleanse the house with holy water and conducted a brief but effective ceremony, after which things settled down and went right back to normal.

Also joining us for our investigation of Bodmin Jail are Lesley and Gaynor, two relatively new investigators who make up for their lack of experience with a willingness to learn and an enthusiasm for all things paranormal that is second to none. We will also be joined for one night by Caroline, a nurse who had joined Lesley, Stephen, and I for our 2015 investigation into the bizarre goings-on at the Cage, a former prison for those accused of witchcraft in the small town of St. Osyth, Essex.

Before setting out for our first night at Bodmin Jail, our small group of friends gathers for a hot dinner at the Jamaica Inn. Alcohol is strictly off the menu, which is our policy on all paranormal investigations; there can be a great deal of subjectivity involved, including personal experiences that are difficult or impossible to verify, and adding alcohol into the mix would only serve to invalidate them completely. Despite the excellent selection of ales at the bar, we stick to tea, coffee, and soft drinks instead. With jet lag working against us, Stephen and I are going to be leaning heavily on caffeine to get ourselves through the next few nights.

There's a feeling of almost indescribable excitement emanating from everybody gathered around the table. I'm digging into the best steak and ale pile I've had in years and simply enjoying being in the company of my friends. For me, this is one of the best parts of any paranormal journey: everybody coming together at the outset, eagerly anticipating the adventure that is still to come. The nights ahead are full of mystery and potential, and we're really hoping that Bodmin Jail will live up to its incredible reputation.

Although we will sometimes be using Gaynor and Caroline's personal cars for traveling between the Jamaica Inn and Bodmin Jail, we also have occasion to make a couple of taxi journeys. When they hear where we're going, it turns out that each of the two drivers has their own ghost story concerning the jail, and they are both only too willing to share their experiences with us.

The first driver, a former Royal Marines Commando who says that he had served in Afghanistan, makes no bones about having been more than a little creeped out by the place. He reveals that he had once taken his dog to the jail for a day's outing. Everything had been just fine until they came to the condemned prisoner's cell. This was a cell used for those who were about to die. When I first come across the cell myself later that night, I expect to find that it was the place where the condemned were imprisoned the day and night before their execution; in fact, most prisoners were kept in there for at least three weeks, simply because the laws at the time mandated that a prisoner scheduled for imminent execution must be allowed a minimum of three consecutive Sundays before the sentence was carried out. In practice, this meant that an inmate would have plenty of time to become acquainted with this 'temporary' cell before their life was cut short at the end of the hangman's rope.

"My dog started going berserk when we got to that cell," the driver recalls, "acting like there was something invisible in there that I couldn't see. Her hackles went up and she was staring at a fixed spot in the room. I practically had to drag her away. When I got talking to a couple of other dog owners later on that same afternoon, both of them told me their dogs had been fine until they reached the Condemned Cell, and then they'd gone ballistic."

He then goes on to tell us that he had been called to the jail once to pick up a distraught visitor who had been taking a night-time ghost tour. The guest had been an absolute wreck, sobbing that they just couldn't take being inside the jail for even a minute longer. There was no specific reason for this sudden onset of fearfulness, but it was nonetheless strong enough to have caused the visitor to flee the building and wait outside the front gates for the taxi to arrive.

The second driver's story turns out to be every bit as interesting. Back in the day, the jail was once a nightclub and casino known as 'The 99 Club' (it's pithy tagline: 'the Clink with a Drink') and one day he happened to be visiting. Sitting at a table and minding his own business, the driver could hardly believe his eyes when he watched a tablecloth suddenly whip itself off from its table and go flying halfway across the room.

"I got up and went to have a look at it, wanting to make

sure that nobody was messing me around," he tells us, "but when I picked it up, there was no fishing wire attached to it or anything like that. Nobody was playing silly buggers. To this day, I couldn't tell you how it happened…just that it *did*."

Bodmin is a picturesque Cornish town situated close to Bodmin Moor, with narrow, winding streets and plenty of hills. All the taxi cab drivers are very familiar with the jail. When ours drops us off outside the big main gate, he offers me a cheery smile and says, "Good luck — you're going to need it…"

I pay and tip him, then go around to the back of the car and start unloading our equipment cases. The jail is located on a hill with a fairly steep slope, overlooking the land around it from a very commanding position. The huge stone walls are cold and intimidating, just as prison walls are supposed to be. The main entrance to the jail is served by a large gatehouse. Although it's the end of the day, the stout wooden doors are standing wide open. Our first sight of Bodmin Jail makes it seem distinctly uninviting, and we walk inside, following in the footsteps of countless former prisoners, with no small sense of trepidation.

CHAPTER THREE
Haunted History

The sense of history that the old jail exudes is so strong, it's almost palpable. As our adventure begins, I'd like to share a little of that history with you first.

During the second half of the 18th century, Cornwall's jails were getting overcrowded. Bodmin itself had a sheriff's ward, a jailing facility which was primarily a jail for debtors. At the time of writing, the old sheriff's ward is now a pub named *The Hole in The Wall* (or simply *The Hole* to the locals). There was also a House of Correction, which is no longer standing. Even combined, the two facilities lacked the capacity to handle the number of people being sentenced by magistrates to serve time behind bars.

In 1778, an Act of Parliament was established by royal decree of King George III, *"for building an additional Jail, and alfo a Prifon and Houfe of Correction, within the County of Cornwall."* Bodmin, according to the wording of the act, *"being, from its situation, and the advantages of healthy air, a good soil, and plenty of pure and wholefome water, efteemed the propereft place for the erection of fuch additional or new jail."*

The new institution was intended to be a big step up from the established standard. The health of the inmates (and jailers) was to be of prime importance, so it would be designed with an eye toward good air circulation. This was achieved via the equivalent of central heating, thanks to a huge stove that was located down in the depths of the structure. Heated air was distributed throughout the building via a system of ducts and vents, before leaving the jail by way of the tall plenum tower which acted as a chimney.

Hygiene was also crucial — infectious disease often ran rampant through crowded prison populations. Clean, running water would help with that, and it would be piped directly into each of the communal courtyards. Hot water came from boilers, which allowed the prisoners to wash, shave, and take regular baths, and an infirmary was constructed in order to care for those who became sick.

When it came to the inmates, the population of Bodmin Jail was to be divided into three broad categories. The first were the felons, long-term offenders who could spend years-long stretches incarcerated there. Some would spend more of their lives behind the walls of Bodmin Jail than they did as free men and women in the world outside.

The second group of prisoners were the misdemeanants,

those who had been convicted of relatively minor offenses requiring shorter spells behind bars. Lastly came the debtors. In some parts of the country, they had their own dedicated prisons, but in Cornwall, space was apportioned for them in the newly-appointed Bodmin Jail. These were men and women who had failed to repay money that they owed, bankruptcy having far more severe consequences in the 1700s and 1800s than it does today.

In addition to the three different groupings of prisoners, they would be further subdivided into male and female offenders. There was to be no intermingling of the genders at Bodmin Jail, and female guards were on hand to manage the female prisoners.

It was a commonly-held belief that a prison had to do more than simply imprison and punish its inmates. Prisoners should be given meaningful work, the popular line of thinking went, and so they were made to earn their keep by performing several different forms of manual labor. They were worked hard in an attempt to get them to see the error of their ways. Down in the basement of Bodmin Jail was (and still is) a device known as the treadwheel or treadmill, which is not dissimilar in concept to the exercise devices we use today. The treadwheel was a huge drum which was designed to revolve when prisoners stepped on its treadboards. Prisoners who were sentenced to hard labor found themselves doing fifteen-minute stretches on the wheel throughout the course of the day. Once their fifteen minutes was up, they would sit down and pick oakum, a type of tarred fiber used to caulk the hulls of ships. Oakum made at Bodmin Jail was sold to shipbuilders at a tidy profit and helped pay for the upkeep of the jail.

One can only imagine how much the prisoners' legs and fingers ached after spending a day going back and forth between the treadwheel and picking oakum. It would certainly have been no picnic. Climbing the wheel was done in total solitude — each prisoner was isolated from their neighbors on either side by wooden screens — and in absolute silence. The combination of boredom and monotonous exertion must have been mind-numbing, to say the least. Male prisoners could also be made to break rocks and beat ropes, whereas their female counterparts were put to work stitching, sewing, and washing.

Between the years 1735 and 1909, eighty people were executed in Cornwall. Predictably enough, the most common reason by far was murder. Thirty-three prisoners were hanged for that particular crime. The second most common reason was burglary (thirteen hangings, although they ended in 1828). Infanticide — the murder of a baby or young child — and highway robbery came next, both tied with seven executions apiece.

The theft of various items, usually livestock, were also the causes of hangings. Two prisoners were hanged for forgery, and two more for arson. One man even danced at the end of a rope for the rather embarrassing crime of bestiality.

Of those eighty executions, a significant number took place at Bodmin. Yet not all of them took place within the walls of the jail itself. Until 1802, executions (which were usually a public affair) took place on Bodmin Common. The venue was then moved to a place just outside the wall of the old jail, where they remained until 1834, when executions began to occur inside the grounds of Bodmin Jail.

There were three different hanging sites within the perimeter of the jail. Two were located out by the walls, close to the Naval Wing — eleven prisoners were executed between those two places. In 1901 came the hanging pit (also known as the execution shed), a dedicated gallows and trapdoor apparatus that was constructed adjacent to the stable shed. Only two prisoners were ever hanged there, but as my team and I were to discover, the atmosphere in that part of the jail grounds has to be experienced to be believed.

The new jail served its purpose well, but when the Napoleonic Wars came to an end in 1815, it soon became stretched beyond its capacity to readily accommodate prisoners. Soldiers and sailors found themselves cast ashore, discharged from a military that no longer needed their services. Many flocked to Cornwall, where the mining business was booming, in the hope of building a better life. More people naturally meant more crime, and the prison population soon began to swell.

One of the strangest and most grisly deaths to take place at Bodmin Jail happened on August 16, 1839. A police constable was escorting a new prisoner to the jail from one of the surrounding villages. No sooner had they reached sight of their final destination than the man, one Thomas Werry, somehow contrived to cut his own throat. Despite efforts to save his life, the would-be inmate bled to death before ever setting foot inside the jail.

In 1827, the jail was the scene of a riot when an unruly mob of male prisoners refused to carry out their assigned duties of hard labor on the treadwheel. When push came to shove, they began smashing up the wooden railings and using the broken remnants as weapons.

For their part, the prison authorities were not willing to waste any time negotiating with what they saw as a bunch of ruffians. They turned out the local militia, who promptly descended on Bodmin Jail and assembled in battle formation inside the courtyard. The sight of ranks of troops bearing muskets and rifles ought to have cowed the rioters, but in fact it had quite the opposite reaction: they charged outside, hooting and hollering as they ran straight at the astonished soldiers.

It is nothing short of a miracle that no shots were fired or prisoners bayonetted to death. Instead, showing an unusual degree of restraint and self-discipline, the militiamen put their weapons to good effect as clubs, beating the rowdy prisoners into submission and then herding them back to their cells. The ringleader, who went by the name of Sowden, remained belligerent and uncooperative, and so magistrates gave the order to have him whipped in front of all the other prisoners. This brutal punishment, which often tore the flesh of the recipient's back into bloody strips, provided a very strong lesson in the cost of disobeying authority. Sullen and grumbling but with their obedience now restored, the remaining inmates grudgingly went back to work. The riot was effectively put down without any cost in lives.

The Naval Prison branches off from the body of the main jail. At the time of our visit, it is crumbling and long-abandoned. After 1878, it was used to house Royal Navy sailors who were convicted of imprisonable crimes. Conditions inside the Naval Prison were strict. The men's daily routine was run to a very high standard of discipline, because those who commanded the Senior Service did not want it to be seen as a soft, easy option for sailors seeking to shirk their duty. A holiday from military service it most definitely was not. The men were worked hard and kept long hours, though they were fed relatively well in comparison to civilian prisoners.

In 1911, the section of Bodmin Jail dedicated to housing female prisoners was shut down. Following the outbreak of World War I in 1915, the number of people being sentenced to prison time plummeted. The main jail itself was shut down in 1916, followed by the Naval Prison in 1922. Yet although its time as an operational prison was at an end, there was life in the old place yet. The various buildings were put up for sale, and there was no shortage of potential buyers.

During the 1930s, it became a place of tourism, where mock executions were carried out for the curious visitors at least four times a day. For the princely sum of one shilling, members of the public could visit and see exactly how some of Bodmin Jail's prisoners would have met their ultimate end.

Another World War came in 1939, and Bodmin Jail found itself hosting the irreplaceable crown jewels, which were kept in the Condemned Cell under heavy guard.

As the years went on, the jail underwent a complete transformation, becoming a night club and casino. *Come to Cornwall's Gayest Night Spot*, one of the advertising fliers trumpeted. *The only place in Cornwall where you can see two different first-class cabaret acts twice nightly, seven nights a week, and dancing!* The same flier proudly announces the double bill of Paul Daniels *("must be one of the best comedians and magicians in the business")* and *Striptease by Farina*. A far cry from the days of imprisonment and hanging.

Have You a Convict's Number? asks a different flier for *the 99 Club*, The Old Prison, Bodmin. *If not, you are cordially invited to apply for same at the above!!!!* The club offered membership cards for customers, and promised that

You'll Never Want Bail When You Come to Our Jail!

With such a rich and colorful history, much of it tainted with death and negativity, no wonder people say that Bodmin Jail is haunted. The only question I have is: just how much of it is true?

I'm determined to find that out for myself.

CHAPTER FOUR
Apparition in the Cellar

Crossing the open space between the gatehouse and the main jail building itself, I notice that there are several smaller buildings situated off to both the left and the right. We'll become better acquainted with them all as the investigation goes on.

A small flight of stone steps leads up to the jail proper. Heading inside, we take a right turn and find ourselves in the tea rooms, where we meet our hosts for the night: Mark and Kirsten, who run regular public paranormal events at the jail.

Mark is a middle-aged gentleman with a stocky build and a serious affect, though it is by no means cold or unfriendly. Kirsten, a dark-haired woman who likes to dress in black, is a little more intense. Introductions are made, handshakes are exchanged, and as the duo lead my fellow investigators and I back into the depths of the jail, it becomes very apparent that they are both very protective of the place and the spirits that they claim still haunt it.

We get a whistle-stop tour of each floor, but Kirsten and Mark are careful to give us little in the way of detail. They have elected to leave us pretty much alone for the first few hours of our investigation. Their rationale for doing so is a simple one and makes eminent sense: neither one of them wants to prejudice my team and I by planting ideas in our heads that might unduly influence us.

"We'll come and join you for the rest of it," Mark promises, "but first I want you to get your feet wet without any interference from us."

I tell him that I appreciate their approach, and then ask Kirsten — who has identified herself as a sensitive — how the energies in the building feel to her tonight. What I really mean is, are the spirits going to be active?

"This building is *always* active," she replies archly. "The entities are out in force tonight, and they're interested in you newcomers and whatever it is that you're going to do. *Very* interested…"

"Brilliant." I clap my hands together, full of enthusiasm. Here we are in what is arguably Britain's most haunted jail, we have the whole place pretty much to ourselves, and according to one of the resident experts, the spirits are already starting to take an interest in us. I can hardly wait to get things rolling.

"They're fascinated by the fact that there's an American here," she adds, looking directly at Stephen, who offers her a courtly bow of the head in acknowledgment.

"Two, actually," I point out. After living in the States for almost twenty years, I now have dual nationality. I like being a son of both worlds.

"You don't count," Kirsten shoots back with a half-smile. "You were born in Leicester."

"Twenty years removed, though."

She rolls her eyes. "You know what I mean. He's a *proper* American."

"I was deported," I joke, "for my crimes." This is a reference to the punishment of *transportation,* in which a prisoner could be sentenced to be forcibly sent to the colonies in lieu of execution. If any of the spirits that haunt Bodmin Jail had been sent to America during their lifetime, the chances were that they didn't go willingly — with one possible exception. Murderer William Hampton, who had strangled his fiancee to death in a sudden fit of rage, had once traveled to America as a young man before returning to his roots back home in Cornwall. I wondered if he might make some kind of connection with Stephen or myself, another Englishman who had gone to America and then returned to the mother country. Stranger things had happened.

There's just one thing I want to hear more about before we kick off our investigation: the infamous video.

When Southampton-based paranormal investigator Tony Ferguson made public a piece of video footage that he had taken at Bodmin Jail, it didn't take long for it to go viral. According to newspaper accounts, Tony and his wife were filming down in the basement, covering the length of one of the longer corridors.

The footage shows what appears to be the ghostly figure of a man walking from right to left through a doorway at the far end of the corridor. According to the media, who picked up on the story and ran with it, Mr. Ferguson may have captured on film the apparition of that very same William Hampton, the last man ever to be executed at the jail.

After reviewing the footage on YouTube, I conclude that Tony Ferguson may indeed have caught something paranormal on camera down in the basement of Bodmin Jail. Staff at the jail have confirmed that there was nobody else wandering through the building when he and his wife were conducting their investigation. But is this really the apparition of William Hampton, or could it be one of the jail's many other resident spirits?

Mark and Kirsten are absolutely convinced that the

video footage is legitimate. They lead us down to the basement and take us to the exact same spot in which Tony and his wife had been standing at the time. I stand there for a moment, peering at the same doorway through which the mysterious figure had been briefly visible. Mark and Kirsten then make their case for the apparition being that of somebody other than William Hampton.

"The video was taken on the anniversary of one of our executions," Mark begins, "but it wasn't that of William Hampton — it was William *Bartlett*. It also happened at about the same time that the real execution would have taken place. The entity was heading toward the area of the prison graveyard. This isn't the route that the condemned man would have taken on his way to the gallows."

"We don't believe that the apparition was anything to do with William Hampton or any of the other former prisoners," Kirsten adds. "It makes more sense to us that it would be a priest, or perhaps one of the warders. Personally, I think it's a priest, because the figure looks as though it's wearing a robe."

It's an interesting theory, and I resolve to devote some time to conducting EVP sessions in that same location in an attempt to try and gather some supporting evidence.

"There's another aspect of the footage that strongly suggests it is genuine," she goes on, "and it's something that Tony Ferguson couldn't have known at the time he filmed it. If you look at the height of the figure's head, it seems to be very far off the ground."

I re-run the video on my tablet. She is absolutely right. The figure would have to be somewhere in the region of seven-and-a-half to eight feet tall if it was walking at the current ground level. That's strange, even for a supposed apparition.

"But the thing is, the floor used to be higher there. The level has been brought down since then. Anybody walking through that corridor back when the prison was still running would have been standing about a foot or so higher than they would today."

Now, that *was* interesting. The seven of us — Mark, Kirsten, Stephen, Lesley, Gaynor, Caroline and I — all go over to see for ourselves. I'm fairly tall at 6'3" and my head doesn't even come close to the same height as that of the figure in Tony's video.

I retrace the figure's footsteps while the others watch and take pictures for comparison. My head dips and bobs, due to the fact that I have to walk down several steps, traverse a straight section of corridor directly adjacent to the doorway, and then climb back up several more steps to reach the next stretch of hallway. The person in the video should, if they had been a flesh-and-blood human being, have done exactly the same thing, yet they hadn't…they had walked straight across thin air without so much as skipping a beat.

It shouldn't have been possible, but there it was on video for all to see.

Something else that impresses me about the video footage is that Tony Ferguson had brought it to Mark and Kirsten straight away, as soon as he had discovered it. I am always rather doubtful of those people who leave a haunted location, only to return at a later time with a spectacular piece of video or photographic evidence that they had only just 'discovered.' Yes, the evidence review process takes time (ask any paranormal investigator, and they'll tell you that it's the most time-consuming part of the whole endeavor) but that time can sometimes be used by those who are less than scrupulous to doctor up something spectacular. It's amazing how far a little skill in Photoshop or other video graphic manipulation techniques can go. Such fakes circulate around the Internet and make news daily. The fact that Tony Ferguson took his findings to Mark and Kirsten almost immediately diminishes the likelihood of his having altered the footage in any way — not to mention the fact that there are video cameras mounted down in the basement that would probably have caught him doing so anyway, had he been unwise enough to try.

Tony was completely up-front with what he had found, showing Kirsten and Mark the footage in its raw, unedited state. They found absolutely no reason to doubt its validity whatsoever. Thanks to the CCTV camera footage, they could also say with certainty that nobody else other than Tony and his wife had been down in the basement of the jail at that time. There was no way that the figure on the video could be anything other than an apparition.

"I've worked here for thirteen years, and Kirsten has worked here for three," Mark tells us, "and contrary to what the papers sometimes say, nothing shocks us. *Nothing.* We've both experienced a lot. But this is one of the most impressive pieces of evidence that we've ever seen come out of this jail."

Something about the mention of CCTV cameras makes me stop and think for a moment. I put it to our hosts that with a network of electronic eyes watching the jail 24 hours per day, 7 days per week, 365 days per year, surely a bunch of unusual sightings must come up? They reply that yes, indeed there are a number of very strange things that have cropped up on the camera feeds, including various light anomalies (not to be confused with the ubiquitous so-called 'orbs' that can in most cases be explained away as dust particles), inexplicably swirling mists, and even the occasional shadow figure. The problem was that barring a security-related emergency, which are thankfully few and far between, there was never really a need to watch all those countless hours of CCTV camera footage…and neither was there the manpower to review it all. I can't help wondering whether the stored video files were actually a treasure trove of unrecognized paranormal activity; treasure that was lost to the world every time the hard drives were written over.

Because of how credible Mark and Kirsten feel that his video capture is, I decide to call Tony Ferguson myself so that I can hear his side of the story in his own words.

Tony confirms that he and his wife were the only two people present in the basement at the time. They spent two hours there in total, between 11am and 1pm. The two of them were filming, Tony was calling out to any spirits that were willing to interact with him, when all of a sudden, the lights were switched out — by who, nobody knows. Neither of them expected to be plunged into near-darkness, but they kept shooting and asking questions. Mark and Kirsten confirmed that they were not responsible for hitting the light switch, and nobody else was on the staircase or in the basement at the time.

"When the lights went out, I could see a figure standing at the end of the hallway," Tony recalls. "There was a whooshing sound as it went past the camera. When I looked at the footage afterward with headphones on, I found that the word 'rape' is also spoken quite clearly. Neither my wife or I said that word. I mean, why would we?"

The big question that Tony and his wife had was: Was this something residual, or could it have been intelligent? "I think it was intelligent," he says, adding that "residual spirits can't switch the lights out." He's convinced that the same spirit was following them both around the jail during their visit.

"I don't think it was negative, but I did feel that it was very pissed off at me for some reason. Bodmin's a jail, and in jails, there's always an alpha male. I'm quite a big lad, so maybe it felt threatened."

He's also open to the possibility that the figure could have been a priest, mainly due to the robe it appeared to be wearing, but it's difficult to understand where the word 'rape' would connect to that.

Our conversation leaves me with much to mull over, but most of all, it tells me that we'd be wise to pay a lot of attention to this part of the jail during our stay.

"The video footage is impressive, but there must be some incredible audio captures too," Stephen prompts, and Kirsten relates the story of a recent conversation that she and Mark had been having, one in which an invisible third party had decided to throw in their two cents' worth.

They had been casually chatting away while setting up some recording equipment, idly discussing a question that centered around the semantics of execution: Was the condemned prisoner 'hung' or were they 'hanged?' (Now that Kirsten poses the question, I am ashamed to admit that I have no idea which one it was — so much for me being a professional writer).

As they bantered back and forth, neither one of them heard anything out of the ordinary, yet when they played the audio recording back, the sound of a man's voice could be heard to speak one single word: *"Hanged..."*

The residents of Bodmin Jail are never shy about making their opinions known, she assures us with a twinkle in her eye.

    I truly hope that she's right.

CHAPTER FIVE
"You Don't Really Know Him."

Mark gives us a hand-held radio and sets it to the same frequency as his own. He and Kirsten promise to lock us all inside the building, adding that they will both hang out upstairs in their office at the top of the tower and keep well out of our way. If we need anything, or feel like taking a break and happen to need access to the outside of the jail, all we have to do is call them on the radio. With a smile and a wave, they head off for the comforts of the office, leaving the five of us — Stephen, Lesley, Gaynor, Caroline, and I — to our own devices.

"Where do you want to start?" Gaynor asks, eager to be off and running.

"Down in the basement," I respond without hesitation. This is where Tony Ferguson's apparition had been caught on video, after all, and the basement is by all accounts an exceptionally active part of the jail.

Gathering up our equipment, we head for the staircase that leads down into the bowels of the jail. As we descend, I keep my head on a swivel at all times. Ever since first setting foot in the jail, there has been a definite sense of being watched. The rational part of my mind knows, of course, that this is almost certainly a psychological phenomenon — when you're in an old dark building in the vicinity of which so many people have died, and one that has a reputation for being extremely haunted, you are already psychologically predisposed to interpret every strange flicker of shadow, every creak or random tap, as the presence of some kind of phantom. But then there's that other part of our brain, the part of us all that is millennia old and still fears the things that our imagination tell us are lurking in the darkness; it's already whispering that even though there might be a perfectly normal, everyday explanation for all of that stuff, it doesn't necessarily mean that the ghosts *aren't* there as well, silently watching us — and getting ready to make their presence known whenever they feel like it. Kirsten certainly seems to think so, and it's going to be interesting to see whether she's right or not.

The staircase is steep and narrow, not to mention potentially treacherous in the low-light conditions. I go first, using a flashlight to guide us, keeping one hand on the curving wall to my left in order to give a little extra support. The sound of our breathing competes with the echo of five sets of footsteps in the enclosed stairway, and I can easily imagine generations of prison guards climbing up and down these same steps as they went about their assigned duties.

After what seems like forever, I reach a landing at the bottom of the staircase and set out in a random direction. The basement level of the jail is slightly dank, a result of the cold water that permeates the rock on which it stands. It also feels decidedly unwelcoming. We select a room in which three very life-like mannequins are posed in such a way as to simulate a double-hanging. One, a bald man who is presumably meant to be the executioner, has been positioned with both hands resting on top of the lever that would send the other two mannequins through the trapdoor of the mock gallows they are standing on. The fact that one of the two soon-to-be-hanged dummies has a sack over its head makes it even creepier, particularly when we go lights-out a few minutes later.

"Ladies and gentlemen," I solemnly intone, taking out my phone and holding it up. "Please join me for the ceremonial shutting down of the cell phones."

Each of us makes a point of putting our phones and tablets into airplane mode so that they will generate no stray signals; otherwise there is a very real likelihood of them triggering the EMF (electromagnetic field) meters that we use to rule out natural and artificial sources of electromagnetic energy when taking baseline readings, which happens to be our first task. We soon figure out where the peaks and troughs of EMF are in the room, and make a note of their locations to act as reference points later on.

EMF can be a funny thing sometimes. Some people think that the presence of unexplained spikes on a K-2 or Tri-field EMF meter signals the presence of a spirit or some other discarnate entity. This theory has never been proven, though it does not lack for supporters— the jury is still out, so far as I am concerned, though I tend to come down on the side of the skeptics in this case. But what we *can* say with real confidence is that high levels of electromagnetic energy can affect the brain in strange ways (such as inducing hallucinations and other bizarre feelings if the energy field is strong enough) and so it is best to find a place to sit or stand that is well away from any major EMF spikes.

On a brief side note, it has also been theorized that strong EMF fields may act as a potential source of fuel for spirit entities, allowing them to use all of that free energy in order to manifest paranormal phenomena. Over the course of my own career as a paranormal investigator, I have come to believe that there may well be some merit to this idea. With the exception of the outdoor wings, which are currently under renovation, Bodmin Jail does not lack for electrical power, and I wonder whether the indoor sections will be more active than those that lacked electrical wiring.

I start my digital voice recorder running and set it down in the center of the room. The five of us spread out, either lounging against the wall or sitting down on the cold stone floor, and make ourselves as comfortable as we can.

We kick things off with a burst EVP session. This is a very simple technique in which the investigator makes a brief audio recording, lasting anywhere from thirty seconds to two minutes, during which they ask questions of any spirits who might be present.

Gaynor starts, introducing herself in a polite manner that wouldn't have been out of place at a garden party. She and I spent several years lugging radios around the countryside as soldiers in the same Territorial Army unit, and her courteous, no-nonsense attitude is a great asset to the team.

Unfortunately, when we play back the burst session, the only responses to her friendly questions are the rumblings of various stomachs, a reminder that we haven't eaten since leaving the Jamaica Inn earlier that afternoon.

Suddenly, shuffling noises coming from the far end of

the corridor make Gaynor pause. "I'd swear somebody's moving around down there at the other end of that hallway," she whispers, craning her neck around the doorway to try and get a better look.

The door to our room looks directly out onto the corridor where Tony Ferguson had recorded his video. Getting carefully to my feet, I sneak out into the hallway, flashlight in hand, and shine the beam down its full length. I play the beam across the walls, floor, and even the ceiling.

Needless to say, there's nothing there.

"Maybe it's a trick of the light," Gaynor says, not sounding very convinced.

A few minutes later, Stephen sees something moving in the darkness out there — the sighting is fleeting, lasting just for a brief second, and may well have been a trick of the light, but we have to consider the possibility that it could also have been something entirely different.

I change position in order to give myself a clearer view of the doorway, and as the EVP session goes on, I also catch sight of movement at the end of the hallway.

Switching my flashlight back on, I make my way all the way down to the end of the corridor and take a good look around. Other than the occasional drip of water, everything is still and quiet. Perhaps our eyes and ears have been playing tricks on us, but if so, then three members out of my team of five have been affected. It seems as though this particular hallway bears watching a little more closely.

"What I saw was a figure," Stephen insists, "a very *dark* figure. Do you see that small light up there?" He indicates a red L.E.D. that's mounted high up on the wall. It's either a security camera or part of the fire alarm system, by my reckoning. We all nod. "It walked right past that, and blotted it out, just for a second."

"Wait a minute," I say slowly, "if this figure of yours managed to somehow blot out that light, it would have to be at least eight or nine feet tall. Maybe even *ten.*"

"Yeah," the priest replies, nodding his head, "or standing on a level of the floor that was a couple of feet higher than it is today."

That reminds us once again of Tony Ferguson's apparition, and how it had also seemed to be walking on a higher level of flooring than what was actually there today. Coincidence, or something more?

There's only one way to find out. Grabbing our equipment, all five of us decide to relocate, heading down toward the far end of the corridor where Stephen had first caught sight of the figure.

We settle down in our new positions and begin to ask more questions. A loud clanking or banging sound startles us all. It seems to have come from the opposite end of the hallway, from the very same area that we had only just left. The noise was loud, distinct, and possibly artificial in nature; it sounded almost as if somebody had hit the wall with an object of some sort. We all look at one another. There hadn't been a peep when we were sitting in that room only a few minutes earlier, but the instant we relocate, suddenly there is an unexplained noise. That seems awfully coincidental to me, but it could still have a perfectly natural explanation.

When I review the audio files afterward, I discover that the sound had been recorded very clearly, and was totally different from the regular dripping of water. Several similar noises follow, all of them seeming to originate from that same end of the hallway. The noises gain in speed, beginning to come faster and faster. In the end, I write them off as most probably having an artificial origin of some kind, although we never did figure out exactly what it was. The sounds are too regular, too methodical, to be anything else, which makes a conventional explanation far more likely than a paranormal one.

Suddenly, apropos of nothing, a chill runs through me, making me shiver. "Somebody just walked over my grave," I say, doing my best to make light of it. We're in a dank and drafty stone basement, so even bundled up in warm clothing as we are, the likelihood of us getting cold is fairly high. What seems strange about *this* particular sensation, however, is that it somehow manages to affect my entire body from head to toe, all at the same time, and then disappears as quickly as it arrived. I feel absolutely frozen to the bone for about four or five seconds, and then things go right back to normal again. There's very little airflow down in the basement of the jail, something I prove with a handy high-tech piece of paper (my preferred method of checking for drafts). At the time, I come down on the side of skepticism and conclude that this highly subjective personal experience is best written off as nothing more than a freak draft. Looking back on it with the benefit of hindsight, however, I am not quite so sure that it wasn't an early sign of things to come...

We run a second EVP burst session that's a little over two minutes long. Unlike the first session that we had conducted in the room with the three mannequins, this one yields actual results. As we gather together around the recorder, straining to hear the playback, we all hear something that hadn't been audible the first time around.

"What was that?" Lesley demands. "Play it back again."

Stephen hooks up the recorder to an external speaker and cranks up the volume as far as it will go without distorting the audio beyond all recognition.

"Will it come on automatically?" Gaynor is heard to ask on the playback, referring to the audio recorder. A soft, breathy male voice immediately whispers in response, "*No.*"

"Was that any of you?" Gaynor asks, looking from Stephen to Caroline to myself, and back again. We all shake our heads. Neither Stephen or I are really 'breathy whisper' sort of guys, and Caroline is always very quiet. We make a point of not whispering during an investigation as a matter of standard protocol, primarily because whispers are almost impossible to distinguish from EVPs during playback. All of which begs the question, just who exactly *had* answered Gaynor?

Nor is that all. On the strength of this rather impressive EVP, we decide to try another burst session. Rather than ask direct questions, though, we agree to just sit around and chat for the duration of it, "shooting the shit" as Stephen likes to call it. One thing that Stephen and I have both found to be true is that it is possible to try *too* hard during a paranormal investigation. If you are too pushy, too focused on getting results at all costs, then quite often you end up with nothing at all. It is almost as if we throw up some sort of psychic or mental block when we attempt to force things to happen. Sometimes, just going with the flow is the approach that yields the best results.

Stephen and I spend a couple of minutes idly discussing the goings-on in the paranormal research community, particularly a recent investigation that had been conducted by a mutual acquaintance of ours. This person happens to be a friend of Stephen's, but somebody I have only met once, briefly, and barely know at all.

When we play the conversation back, it appears as though our invisible companion — or possibly one of his friends — had also wanted to put in his two cents' worth again.

On the audio recording, you can hear me say the phrase, "I don't really know him well either." The response is immediate, and does not come from Stephen: another male voice, this one with a distinctly Liverpudlian accent, replies, *"You don't really know him."*

This intelligent response nearly knocks our socks off. A

good, clear EVP always makes a long night of investigating well worthwhile all by itself, but too often they are simply random words and phrases. When the EVP appears to either directly answer a question, or comment on something specific that was just said, it adds an entirely new level of validation to the phenomenon. In this case, the unseen speaker also makes a very valid comment. I *don't* really know the researcher in question all that well. The unseen commentator is one hundred percent correct.

Some have argued that EVPs are nothing more than stray radio signals, but what are the odds that over the space of just a few minutes, we would happen to receive *two* supposedly random transmissions that were very clear responses to something that had just been spoken aloud?

We are completely ecstatic about our findings. Kirsten's prediction that the spirits of Bodmin Jail were going to be out and about tonight and taking an interest in our activities, appears to have been validated already. It's good to know that we have at least one invisible participant joining us in the basement of Bodmin Jail tonight.

Now, the question was: will there be more?

CHAPTER SIX
Fed by the Faeries

We're excited to see what the jail has in store for us next. I call up Mark on the walkie-talkie and ask him to unlock a side door, asking him to please let us outside for a bit of fresh air. Lesley needs her inevitable nicotine fix, and we all want to talk about the EVPs. I play the audio recordings back for Mark and Kirsten, neither of whom seems particularly surprised that the jail has already begun to deliver for us.

It's a bitterly cold and clear night, with enough moonlight to highlight the towering stone walls in a pale, silvery glow. Craning my neck, I stare up at the side of the main jail building. The dark windows seem full of mystery and promise, and I feel blessed to have been given the opportunity to spend a little time here, delving into some of the haunted old building's secrets.

Heading back inside, we pause to watch Kirsten close and secure the heavy outer door. We're locked inside the jail again. Lesley starts brewing up some hot tea for those who want a cup, which turns out to be pretty much everybody. In the chilly hallway outside the break room, which is located one floor down from ground level, a space heater is the only thing working to combat the cold.

"Thank you, Tea Wallah." I gratefully accept a Styrofoam tea cup from Lesley, cupping it in both hands. It slowly warms my cold fingers, and I let the steam rise up into my face. It feels comforting and helps to settle my mind.

On the monitor screens, everything seems to be quiet in each security camera's field of vision. There are a few 'orbs' floating past — or, more accurately, dust particles.

Feeling refreshed, we go back downstairs to the basement and try another burst EVP session. There are thuds coming from directly above our heads, the sound of heavy footsteps walking back and forth across the floor. Going over the floor plan of the jail, we determine that the tea rooms are directly above us. That part of the jail, where we met our hosts when we first arrived, has been empty and locked up tight ever since then.

We each take turns introducing ourselves, and invite anybody present to come forward and join in with our conversation. It's another round of our informal chit-chat. Sadly, when we play the audio back, nobody seems to have chimed in.

A few minutes later, we're joined by Kirsten and Mark

once more. Kirsten tells us that there is a male spirit entity standing in one corner of the room — somebody native to the jail, rather than an attachment that one of my team has brought along with us. We're told that he's in his late twenties or early thirties. Stephen has set up a Spirit Box apparatus, and is now fiddling around with the settings.

"He's curious about what you're doing," Kirsten tells him.

"This device takes phonetics from language — a phonetic is part of a word — and it chops them all up," Stephen explains to the unseen onlooker. "The idea is that you put these phonetics back together, in order to *create* words."

I've always been surprised when I watch people on paranormal TV shows visit a historic location, whip out a Spirit Box or some other similar device, and just expect whatever entities might be there to instantly know how to use it. Assuming that you believe such devices truly do communicate with spirits (and the jury is *definitely* still out on that one) then why would we assume that the spirit of somebody who died in, say, the Salem Witch Trials, would automatically know how to manipulate radio waves or electrical signals? Sometimes a little explanation goes a long way.

The device that Stephen is using is more than a little controversial among members of the paranormal research community. Its speaker spits out a fluctuating stream of random noise, snippets of sound which have no inherent meaning, filling the room with gibberish. I, for one, am less than convinced sometimes. There's an echoing reverberation to the quality of the noise which makes the brain *want* to pick out words and phrases from amongst all of the random chaos. In other words, such devices make the listener very susceptible to the phenomenon of *audio pareidolia,* hearing words that aren't really there.

Still, I've always been a big believer in trying out new tools and techniques. Sometimes you get an absolute zinger that will surprise you. I've also heard Spirit Boxes say things that are far too specific to be random, on occasion.

"There's a learning curve," Stephen prompts. "Please keep trying."

Gaynor, Caroline, and Lesley take turns asking a few generic questions. Their hope is that the man Kirsten claims to be seeing might be willing and able to speak with us.

A number of vocal streams start pouring out of the speaker all at the same time, merging into one loud cacophony of noise. None of it is intelligible, but all of it is difficult to listen to. Kirsten adds in some gentle encouragement herself. Mark and I are standing at the back of the room, quietly observing everything that's going on...and keeping a wary eye on the hallway, in case more shadow figures decide to put in an appearance.

The torrent of noise is getting steadily louder and more intense, but it isn't becoming any clearer. I still haven't heard anything that I would classify as a word, let alone a phrase or a sentence.

"Can you say my name?" Stephen asks.

A clear voice responds with *"Phil."* The priest laughs, happy with the reply. He asks whether the voice can say the name *Stephen*. *"Nope,"* comes the reply, earning another chuckle. It sounded very much like the same voice and the same intonation to my ear.

Kirsten asks the speaker whether the guards are kind to him. A heavy, bass *"No, no, no,"* comes through.

Things run on for a little longer, but nothing else of any note emerges. "I think they're getting tired," Stephen says, switching off the device. "I know *I* am. Let's give them a break."

Everybody agrees, and we make our way carefully to the

next location. Lesley remarks that she has started developing a 'pressure-type headache.' This isn't at all uncommon at Bodmin Jail. Numerous visitors have reported experiencing something similar.

As we're making our way back to the break room, I happen to catch sight of Kirsten as she passes from one pool of shadow to another. Her face appears...*strange,* for want of a better term. It seems sinister and aged, like that of an old crone. When I reluctantly mention this – it's hardly the most polite thing for me to say to our hostess – not only does she fail to take offense, but Mark adds that this also happens quite often inside the jail. He personally has seen her face take on a different form, he tells us, and has also heard her voice inexplicably change into that of somebody else. I'm not entirely convinced about what I saw, however. My eyes have got to be playing tricks on me — haven't they?

After a brief discussion, we decide to set up our equipment in what's known as the Faerie Cell. This was said to have once been the cell of a prisoner named Anne Jefferies, whose tale has long been a part of Cornish folklore. As the story goes, Anne was something of a local mystic or wise woman, consorting with the faerie folk and supposedly living with them for several months. Anne had mysterious powers which allowed her to heal the sick and infirm. Finally, threatened by her growing popularity, Anne was thrown into Bodmin Jail by a local magistrate, where she claimed that faeries came to visit her every night, bringing food to sustain her through the long hours of darkness.

It's a wonderful story, and not remotely true — at least, not as far as the Bodmin Jail connection is concerned. References to Anne place her birth in the Cornish town of St. Teath in the year 1626. Even if she had been exceptionally long-lived, there is no way she could possibly have survived long enough to see the construction of Bodmin Jail, let alone become one of its inmates.

Still, it's a beautiful fairy tale (if you will pardon the pun). Stephen sets up his Spirit Box in the hallway directly outside the fairy cell and fires it up, while the rest of us make ourselves as comfortable as we can, leaning against the walls or sitting on the cold stone floor. Fiddling with the volume knob, he cranks the noise level up until the sounds coming through the speaker fill the entire basement.

"We're here to communicate with anybody that wants to talk to us," Stephen announces, opening the session up to all comers. "We ask that you be courteous and respectful, just as we are. We'll ask you a few questions, and you're more than welcome to ask us questions too, if you'd like."

At first, the only intelligible voices we hear seem to be speaking snippets of German. Mark, who has some knowledge of that particular language, points out that a number of German prisoners of war were kept in the Naval Prison during World War One.

"Are there any Germans here?" Kirsten asks.

"Ja!" a voice enthusiastically replies.

"Is Armstrong here?" another voice pipes up, this one speaking English.

(After carrying out some research, we later learn that one Edward Armstrong, a patient at the nearby Cornwall County Asylum, was buried in Bodmin Parish in 1880).

"Mark's here!" exclaims a different voice. All eyes turn toward Mr. Rablin's silhouette. He is standing in the doorway of the Fairie Cell, casually observing everything that's going on. Mark gives a polite nod of the head in the direction of the speaker, acknowledging the shout-out and seemingly unperturbed at being singled out.

"Are you okay down here?" Kirsten wants to know. The response comes straight away: *"No!"* She goes on to explain that some of the cells in the basement are believed to have been communal, rather than single occupancy, and that conditions down here were thought to have been harsher than those on the upper floors.

"Do you know me?" Mark asks. There's no reply.

"Do you know Mark?" chimes in Kirsten. *"No,"* is the instant response.

"Do you know *me?*" Stephen decides to jump on the bandwagon. The answer is again, *"No."*

"Do you want me to help you?" Mark offers. The same surly male voice answers, *"No."*

"Mark," says a different voice, followed by *"Richard."*

"Richard's 'ere!" Lesley says excitedly, her Essex accent growing stronger. "Do you want to speak to 'im?"

"Do I have to?"

The room explodes into laughter. I'm a little embarrassed at have been dissed by a disembodied voice, but at the same time, this degree of interactivity is seriously cool — assuming, that is, that these are genuine discarnate voices and not simply our own ears playing tricks on us and causing our brains to tell us what we want to hear. I try to remain skeptical of this device, as I do of every other tool and technique that we employ in our attempts to investigate the paranormal, but I'm starting to grow impressed nonetheless.

"Do you want us to move to another location?" Stephen enquires once he finally stops laughing. He is rewarded with an emphatic *"Yes."* We return to the room in which we got the *"You don't know him"* EVP earlier on.

Stephen leaves the box running as he carries it along with him. Nothing intelligible comes through it while we're walking along the corridor, but as soon as he enters the cell and sets it carefully on the floor, a voice hisses, *"It's a priest!"*

"Priests may have been a figure of fear for some of the prisoners here," Kirsten points out.

"Stephen is a *nice* priest," I say, trying to placate whoever might be speaking.

"Richard," a different voice pipes up.

I ask how many of those present are Cornish. *"Eight,"* comes the answer. I'm starting to feel impressed. *"F*** off,"* says another. Kirsten gasps, horrified. "Naughty!" she scolds, in the manner of a mother rebuking a misbehaving child.

"Wouldn't be the first time," Mark grins, more amused than shocked. He explains that some of the EVPs and voice phenomena that pop up at Bodmin Jail can be a little on the salty side.

These are the highlights of a session that lasts a little over an hour in total. There's certainly plenty of food for thought as we go to back upstairs to take a break, caffeinate, and use the restroom. Afterward, Mark and Kirsten tell us the sad story of Valeri Giovani, who was the only convict other than William Hampton to be executed in the jail's execution shed. A 31-year-old Italian sailor, Giovani was the very first man to die on the new gallows, hanged in 1901 for the crime of murder on the high seas, after killing one of his shipmates in cold blood.

"My middle name is Giovani," Stephen says quietly once the story has concluded. I'm surprised to hear it, but the priest reassures me that he isn't kidding. That's an interesting piece of synchronicity, an unusual name tying the two men, one living and one dead, together. Kirsten believes that Valeri Giovani is one of the spirits that actively haunts the jail, and when she speaks to him (as she sometimes does) it's with a definite air of affection.

Speaking calmly and with great deliberation, Stephen tells us that while we were just hearing the story, he suddenly got the sense of a relatively young man who was pushed to his wit's end by the fellow sailor that he ultimately turned on.

"He snapped," Mark confirms, "and just lashed out with the closest weapon at hand."

As we're talking, Lesley's flashlight goes dead. The batteries were factory-fresh just a few hours before, and should have lasted for much longer than they have. This sort of thing happens to us all the time at haunted locations, and so nobody is greatly surprised to find that another unexplained battery drain is on the books.

The basement is one of the more active areas of the jail, by all accounts. Both Mark and Kirsten report personal experiences of a physical nature happening to them there. Kirsten once felt herself stroked on the back by an unseen hand, whereas Mark received a rather less pleasant shove while he was leaning against one of the walls. Both occurred when they were relative newcomers to the jail. It may be that the spirits simply hadn't had time to get used to them yet.

I'm wondering whether any of us will be singled our for the same sort of attention.

CHAPTER SEVEN
Warders

While the lowest level of Bodmin Jail has given us some intriguing experiences already, it's a big place, and I'm acutely aware of that fact that we're rapidly burning through our allotted hours of darkness. Not wanting to neglect the rest of the grand old building, I suggest that we head on up to one of the higher floors to see what happens next.

We climb the stairs *en masse,* a chorus of middle-aged bones popping and low moans caused by aching muscles. I glance down at my Fitbit. We're certainly getting the steps in; it's 1:30 in the morning and I'm already at 3,000.

Reaching the central hallway on the ground floor, Stephen fires up an EVP recorder for a burst session and asks that we deploy some E.M. pumps. These little devices flood the environment with electromagnetic energy, which (some have theorized) some entities may be able to use in order to manifest. The theory is totally unproven, but I figure that it's at least worth a try. Some of my colleagues have had good results with the technique in the past.

Midway through the burst session, an ominous growl fills the darkened hallway. All eyes turn toward Stephen, who at least has the decency to look a little embarrassed. His stomach has chosen this moment to misbehave and tell him that it's long overdue for a snack.

The session lasts a little under three minutes, and when we play the audio back, Stephen's gastrointestinal folly is the only thing out of the ordinary that turns up…until the two-minute mark. I'm heard to ask if there are any inmates of the jail present with us tonight, and received nothing but silence. I then expand the question to ask about former warders, guards, or employees. What sounds like a male voice comes immediately afterward. If there were any intelligible words being spoken, they're difficult to make out on first playback, so we hook the voice recorder up to a loudspeaker and play it again. The sound is short — less than two seconds in duration — and seems to whisper the word *"Warders."* It's yet another intelligent and interactive direct response to one of our questions.

Pretty cool, we all agree.

Stephen is looking quizzically at his digital voice recorder. "Dead battery," he explains, shaking his head. "Factory-fresh at the start of the evening."

Another electrical device bites the dust, courtesy of whatever it is that is active at Bodmin Jail. I wonder if there was a connection between the two events — the energy loss and the EVP. Was the electrical power stored within the battery somehow converted into the sound of the EVP, becoming paranormally-imprinted on the recorder's hard drive? It's an intriguing possibility, and one that I find very plausible.

We try another burst session in the same place, asking questions appropriate to the late 19th and early 20th centuries, such as the name of the monarch currently sitting on the throne. Although we don't get any EVPs this time out, all of us hear the sound of shuffling coming from the far end of the corridor. This happens at about the midway-point of the session. The sound is picked up quite distinctly on our recorders, and while it's possibly just a normal background noise, we haven't heard it at all before now, and we don't hear it again afterwards.

"Are you alright?" Caroline, who has been rather quiet so far, asks Lesley. We all turn to look at our favorite investigator/tea-maker. Lesley does not look happy to be here anymore, not one little bit. She has turned pale and seems extremely anxious.

"No," she admits. "I'm scared. *Really* scared. I don't know why, and that's not something that normally happens to me." She's telling the truth. Based on my friendship with Lesley for the past few years, I know her to be a tough-as-nails Essex girl that isn't easily intimidated. She has also put in more than her fair share of time creeping around haunted buildings in the dark with me and the team. If she happened to be prone to getting scared, I would have known about it by now. It's an unusual way for her to behave, something that she readily admits herself.

"Let's go back downstairs for a bit, until you feel better," I suggest. I realize it's the right call to make when Lesley agrees straight away, without even trying to talk me out of it. Normally, she would just blow something like this off and keep on investigating. Instead, she almost looks relieved when we go back to the break room and congregate around the tea urn again. Once her duties as self-proclaimed Tea Wallah have been discharged, she disappears out into the night air to have a cigarette and calm her nerves.

At the time, I'm not giving her reaction too much credence. Maybe, I tell myself, it's just her mood. Everybody gets spooked from time to time, no matter how experienced they are. Hell, I've even felt it myself on a couple of occasions, developing a serious case of the creeps without any apparent reason to explain it away. It will only be later that I will learn there is something within the walls of Bodmin Jail that likes to play mind games with visitors...and that something is not necessarily very nice.

CHAPTER EIGHT
"My God, You've Just Changed..."

In order to break the night up a little bit, we spend some time freely roaming the jail interior. There's no set agenda, just a half-hour of wandering around and getting to know the place a little better. Because of its status as a living museum and tourist attraction, there are a number of mannequins situated in specific parts of the jail. Each is dressed in period-appropriate garb, and the displays help bring to life the story of those who either worked or were imprisoned within the walls of Bodmin Jail over the years

I make sure to visit each one in turn, and try to learn a little about the prisoner's back story. One of the most tragic is the case of Selena Wadge, a child murderess who was hanged at Bodmin in 1878. A single mother of two boys in an age when such a thing was severely frowned upon, Selena had become enamored with a man by the name of James Westwood. She would later make the claim that she and Westwood were going to be married, but only on the condition that one of her children was no longer around.

Unlike his healthy older brother, two-year-old Harry Wadge had a physical disability which meant that he would be unable to care for himself when he grew older. Tragically, he never got the chance *to* grow older, for his mother killed the helpless child by dropping his body into a well while her other son, John, looked on and cried.

She was kept prisoner in the Condemned Cell until the day of her hanging, living under the watchful eye of female guards until the death sentence could be passed. The execution shed had not yet been built. Early on the morning of August 15th, 1878, Selina Wadge plummeted to her death from one of the upper-floor doorways of Bodmin Jail, around which a wooden scaffold had been erected and bolted into the wall. When William Marwood, the executioner assigned to carry out the sentence of death, secured the noose about her neck, Selena uttered her last words: "Lord, deliver me from this miserable world."

A number of visitors to Bodmin Jail claim to have encountered the ghost of Selena Wadge, most often young children who ask their parents about the identity of the crying woman in the long dress that had just swept past them in the hallway. Selena is said to have sobbed and wept bitterly as the guards led her to her death.

Her presence is commemorated at the jail today by a waxwork display, in which she is depicted in the form of a mannequin, dangling a baby over a well by one leg. Another mannequin portrays her eldest son, clutching pathetically at Selina's dress in a feeble attempt to stop her from murdering his little brother.

I stand there for a while, lost in my own thoughts. What frame of mind must a person be in, how desperate would they have to become, in order to drop a helpless child into a well? Not just any child, but *their own* child? Shaking my head in disbelief, I finally walk away.

Selina Wadge is far from being the only murderer who met their demise at Bodmin Jail. Wandering from cell to cell, from floor to floor, I take notes each time I pass a particular cell, and pause awhile to become acquainted with its former occupant. I don't want to forget either their names or their crimes.

One area is mocked up to look like a part of the sailing ship *S.S. Lorton,* the scene of Valeri Giovanni's murder of a shipmate in 1901. A little further along, I come upon the story of William Meagre Bartlett. Despite being married with eight children, Bartlett engaged in an illicit extra-marital affair with a woman who would bear him another child out of wedlock. Rather than confess to adultery and take responsibility for the unwanted pregnancy, Bartlett waited for the baby to be born, and then took it to his place of work: a granite quarry. After strangling the helpless infant with a shoelace, he then threw its body down a deep mine shaft in the hope that it would never again see the light of day.

Perhaps overcome with remorse or an attack of conscience, William Meagre Bartlett attempted to drown himself soon afterward, but without any success. His grisly crime was soon discovered, and after a period of incarceration at Bodmin Jail, he was sentenced to death by hanging. It was recorded that Bartlett offered no resistance whatsoever when he was conveyed from the condemned cell and placed into the custody of the hangman.

In 1812, an innkeeper named William Wyatt murdered a young boy in his bathtub. In 1854, one James Olman battered his wife to death at their home and threw her body into the fire that was burning in the grate. Both men were hanged at Bodmin Jail, as was 27-year-old Robert Brown, who got the rope in 1785 for willfully starving his apprentice boy to death.

Equally tragic is the case of a 22-year-old domestic servant named Elizabeth Commins, who was executed on August 8, 1828. After an illicit sexual liaison with a male servant, Elizabeth found herself to be pregnant. Such a thing constituted a scandal in those days, and so she somehow contrived to keep the pregnancy a secret. Finally, the baby came early one morning, and Elizabeth took herself off to the cow shed in order to give birth, which she did alone and unassisted. As the newborn baby began to cry, she bashed its head against the crib until it was dead. Elizabeth paid for this atrocity with her life.

Another female sentenced to hang at Bodmin was Sarah Polgrean, who fatally poisoned her husband's food with arsenic in 1820. Poisoning was regarded as being a particularly insidious crime at that time, and convicted poisoners often faced the death penalty.

Taking the life of another human being wasn't the only crime for which somebody could find themselves standing atop the hangman's scaffold. I learn a great deal when I stop to browse some of the historical placards that are affixed to the walls. One Elizabeth Osborne was sentenced to death for the crime of arson, after setting fire to a crop of corn. William Wallace (no, not that one) was hanged for stealing a sheep and then killing it. A James Northey was sentenced to execution after breaking into a private residence and stealing the contents — burglary being a potentially capital crime in

1813. Yet, twenty years later in 1833, two rapists named Pascoe and Jenkin were imprisoned at the jail. Despite the public outcry clamoring for them to be hanged, the judge did not sentence them to be executed.

Perhaps the strangest execution on the books at Bodmin Jail was that of William Hocking, a 57-year-old man who was caught having sex with a farm animal, and subsequently hanged on August 21, 1834. As I stand there reading about this truly bizarre crime, two thoughts strike me in rapid succession. The first is that William Hocking was hung on my birthday. The second is simply, *"Ugh."*

Hocking's crime is recreated in the form of a bearded male mannequin that stands nonchalantly in front of a carved wooden sheep. Mercifully, the diorama leaves everything else to the imagination.

As I make my way down the staircase to the basement once again, I revisit one of the rooms that I had found to be particularly intriguing earlier in the night. With the jail's underbelly shrouded in darkness, I head to the room with the double hanging, using my flashlight to guide me on my way.

Two mannequins, one hooded and one bare-headed, have been used to re-create a double hanging which took place outside the jail walls in 1840. The event was considered to be such a public spectacle that more than 20,000 people were said to have attended, clamoring to watch as the Lightfoot brothers (William and James) were hanged for the murder of one Nevill Norway. I cannot help but think that the number must have been an exaggeration, though that is the figure that local newspapers reported at the time. The night before the hanging, every pub in Bodmin was packed full of revelers. The execution itself took place at noon the following day, before a packed mob of baying spectators.

My friends and I gather again in the break room to decide on our next move. We split up, parceling ourselves out between floors in order to minimize the noise pollution and increase our chances of experiencing something strange — or so we hope. I stick with Kirsten, who leads me up to the center of the second-floor hallway. Caroline comes with us.

Kirsten says she is sensing the presence of a very authoritarian personality in this part of the jail, one that is immensely strong and willful. She warns us that it is more than capable of steam-rolling anybody it doesn't like.

"You're saying 'it,' rather than 'he' or 'she,'" I point out. "Are you implying that this energy isn't human?"

Kirsten shakes her head. In the near-total darkness of the hallway, lit only by the emergency lights, her dark black hair gives her a look that's not dissimilar to the creepy girl from the movie *The Ring*. "I think it's the spirit of an inmate, but I'm also picking up on what I think might be something like Multiple Personality Disorder. There are several different energies, but they're all coming from a common source."

Intrigued, I make a note of that. Kirsten pulls across a swinging iron door, separating the hallway into two distinct halves.

"Tell me more about this person you're sensing," I ask her as the door clangs firmly shut. I can't speak for Kirsten and Caroline, but it's hard not to feel a little trapped...which is the whole point of the door, I suppose. The sturdy bars really do make me feel like I'm a prisoner now, and a shiver runs through my body.

"This is somebody with psychopathic tendencies, very prone to violent outbursts. Somebody who would have been a danger to society during their lifetime."

"Which is probably why he ended up here in Bodmin Jail," I reason. She nods.

"Sounds a bit Dr. Jekyll and Mr. Hyde," observes Caroline.

"Where is this entity now?" I ask.

"At the end of the hallway." Kirsten gestures to the far end of the corridor that's closest to us. I turn to look where she's pointing. All I can see is blackness. My heart rate begins to pick up, a reminder that the entity Kirsten claims to be sensing is on the same side of the iron door as we are. Then it suddenly dawns on me just how stupid I'm being; no door ever built could impede a spirit entity, so what does it matter which side of it we're on anyway? There's just that psychological feeling of being trapped, of being shut in to contend with. But Kirsten doesn't seem to be the least bit bothered, and Caroline is her usual inscrutable self, so there's no way I'm letting on to them that I feel a little on edge. I realize that this is nothing more than bravado, which is foolish at the best of times, but there's no way I'm going to let myself get creeped out because I'm locked in a dark prison hallway.

Normally I'd be leaning against the wall and trying to relax, but my senses are all working overtime. I'm feeling hyper-vigilant, picking up on every little sound and flicker of movement. In response to a question from Caroline, Kirsten relates an experience that she had in this same spot during which she seemed to be taken over by the spirit of a

Cornishman, who warned everybody present that 'something' was coming up the stairs.

"I'm going to try a burst EVP session," I announce. Pulling out my recorder, I remark to Kirsten that it would be nice if "you remain you."

"Yes," she deadpans. "It would." There's a gleam in her eye that I can't quite read, but it feels ever so slightly disquieting to me. In fact, it borders on the sinister.

"The atmosphere is getting denser," she tells us. "Darker."

From somewhere in a cell off to Kirsten's left, there comes a light tap. At the same time, I think I catch sight of movement in that same cell. I go inside to look. It's empty. My eyes are playing tricks on me...or so I tell myself.

Sounds bleed up from the floor below. It's Mark and his group moving from one place to another.

"It's gotten very dark in that cell," Caroline says calmly, peering into its depths. I'm always skeptical of those types of claims. The eyes are easily fooled in the dark, after all, particularly when there's little ambient light for them to see by. The mind likes to make up its own random details from the darkness, filling in the blank spots, as it were.

All the same, I'm tempted to agree with her — it really

does seem darker in the cell than it had done earlier. But this could easily be explained away by the power of suggestion. Kirsten now begins to feel nauseous, but she declines my offer to cut the session short and head back downstairs. She tells us that she isn't one for running away from things like this, especially inside the jail. It's important for her to project strength and confidence when she's inside these walls at all times.

"My God, you've just changed on me," she says, with a sharp intake of breath. She's looking straight at me.

"Changed? Changed *how?*"

"Your persona has just switched. Your manner seems very threatening."

I'm puzzled by this. From where I'm standing — just six feet away from her, directly across the corridor — I'm not doing anything differently. My stance and body language are the same, as is my intonation and manner of speaking. Is Kirsten simply imagining things, or could she be right — is it possible that I really *am* beginning to undergo some kind of change? I look at Caroline for confirmation. She shrugs. She doesn't seem to be seeing the same thing that Kirsten is. For my part, I feel perfectly normal.

Just to be on the safe side, I take a step back from them

both.

"You suddenly look as if you're quite a bit taller than you were a few seconds ago," Kirsten adds. This time, Caroline agrees with her, saying that unless she is also seeing things, I *do* appear to have gotten larger in the space of just a few seconds.

"Take a picture," I ask them, closing my eyes against the inevitable flash in order to preserve my night vision. Pulling out their phones, they oblige. I go on over to look at the screens. From what I can see, there's nothing out of the ordinary in either picture. The photographs show me standing just in front of the iron gate, my eyes screwed tightly shut. I certainly don't look any taller than normal. I'm tempted to just chalk this one up to the power of suggestion and the notorious unreliability of the human eye in near-dark conditions. Kirsten and Mark have both told me that other visitors to the jail have reported experiencing the same thing, however, so I resolve to keep an open mind no matter what.

After a while, with nothing more out of the ordinary going on and no attempts at contact from Kirsten's dark entity, we head back downstairs. Caroline seems a little distracted, and confides that she really *did* think I was growing in stature up there. I make a note of it, and resolve to see if anybody else experiences the same thing.

We're all getting tired. Despite the constant flow of caffeine and sugar, I can feel the jet lag starting to bite. Looking at my watch, I can see that sunrise isn't all that far off. Judging from the number of stifled yawns going around the group, we've got maybe one more session left in us before we have to call it a night. Kirsten and Mark escort us to what they call the 'Long Room Corridor.' Bodmin Jail was built in the shape of a cross, and this particular hallway would be the short head of the cross, extending up above the two arms.

Within seconds of one another, Stephen and Kirsten both report sensing the presence of *something,* although they can't say precisely what it is. Spreading out, Stephen starts a short EVP burst session, while I run a second recorder concurrently with his. He speaks conversationally, asking any communicators present if they're willing and able to speak his name. He very explicitly extends the invitation to *positive* spirits only, at first. Then, allowing a few seconds to pass, he perhaps unwisely makes the same offer to any negative entities that might be with us.

"Now back off," he says, wincing and raising his arms defensively. Concerned, I take a step toward him.

"What's going on?"

"I feel as if I'm getting pressed in," he explains, shaking his head slowly from side to side. That makes sense. Expressing a willingness to communicate with negative entities can entail some degree of risk, if you're not very, very careful. We're all going to need to be diligent about our spiritual protection before leaving the jail this morning.

"Try pressing *me,*" I suggest, scowling at my friend's unseen tormentor.

"It won't," Stephen says straight away. "It's focused on me."

The burst session turns up nothing. We linger for a few more minutes, replaying the audio several times over to make sure that we haven't missed anything. Then, by mutual agreement, we call it a night.

After packing up our gear and throwing out the trash, we make our way outside into the courtyard at the front of the jail. The eastern sky is already beginning to brighten. We say our goodbyes to Mark and Kirsten, and afterward, Stephen leads us all in a short ceremony of blessing intended to rid us of any unwanted hangers-on.

Less than an hour later, I'm falling asleep in my bed at the inn. My wife, who had still been fast asleep when I snuck quietly into the room, cocks open one eye and mumbles, "Watch out for the little girl's ghost. She touched me on the ankle last night."

Great, I think to myself as I pull the blankets up to my chin and drift off to sleep. *I hope she's okay with my snoring.*

CHAPTER NINE
The Naval Prison

I sleep like the dead (pun very much intended) for a solid six hours. As you probably know, running on adrenaline and caffeine is a strange thing, especially when you're jet-lagged. One minute you're wide awake, and the next you're so bone-weary you can hardly keep your eyes open. This is the physiologic equivalent of robbing Peter to pay Paul, proving the old saying that there truly ain't no such thing as a free lunch.

Down at the Jamaica Inn bar, the crew all gets together for dinner later that afternoon. Last night's events have left us all excited to go back to the jail and see what's on the menu for tonight. It will be just Stephen, Lesley, and I this evening, as Caroline and Gaynor are sadly unable able to make it.

We pull up outside the jail a little before sunset, and are once again met by Mark, who accompanies the three of us around the main building on a casual stroll. We're just trying to get a feel for the place tonight, to see if the atmosphere feels any different than it did the night before. I can't speak for my companions, but everything seems fine to me.

A commonly-offered explanation for the haunting of some buildings is the so-called 'Stone Tape theory.' Nigel Kneale (of the *Quatermass* TV show fame) is believed to have coined the term for his TV drama of the same name, *The Stone Tape*. Considering that it was made back in 1972 and has special effects that now look decidedly dated, the show has otherwise aged rather well, having lost little of its ability to scare.

The Stone Tape follows the visit of a team of scientists to a supposedly-haunted old building. They are hoping to unlock the secrets of a new method of recording images and sound (the Stone Tape of the title) and as you can probably guess, end up not only proving the theory to be true, but also disturbing a dark paranormal force in the process.

While that is all well and good, *The Stone Tape* is fiction, not fact. Yet Nigel Kneale may well have been on to something. Hauntings do indeed seem to be more prevalent in buildings that are constructed either of, on, or around stone, yet nobody has been able to explain satisfactorily just how the stone might record and then replay ghostly phenomena.

The Stone Tape theory has been largely dismissed by geologists and many of those who are skeptical of the paranormal. It does still have many adherents among members of the paranormal research community, however, and if working in this field for so many years has taught me anything, it is that a theory should not be dismissed out of hand just because we don't have all the answers yet. Time may yet prove either side of the argument to be right; the wise thing to do is to keep an open mind where the theory is concerned.

With that being said, I ask Mark whether he thinks the preponderance of stone in and around Bodmin Jail might account for some of the ghostly activity that is regularly reported there. He believes that it does.

"The jail is roughly 310 feet high and contains over 20,000 tons of granite. If you look closely at the stone itself as we walk around, you'll see lots of quartz. We also have a watercourse running underneath us, which may also be a contributory factor."

Mark is referring to a similar hypothesis to the Stone Tape Theory, which posits that under certain conditions, flowing water or even static pools of water may also be able to act as some form of paranormal recording and playback medium. If one studies the literature of ghosts and hauntings, there certainly does seem to be a correlation between either large bodies of water or fast-moving streams and accounts of ghostly phenomena.

"You also need to look at the fact that there are ley lines beneath the jail too," Kirsten points out.

I raise my eyebrows. Now that *is* interesting. Ley lines are another age-old and relatively controversial concept, believed by some to be subterranean conduits of a type of metaphysical energy whose existence science has yet to acknowledge.

In an article published in *Supernatural Magazine* titled 'Ley Lines and the Connection to Adverse Spiritual Phenomena,' author Clare Lewis makes the intriguing claim that two such ley lines can be found directly beneath Bodmin Jail.

...most of the Earth's leys are positive, but when two of these leys cross or intersect a vortex of negative energy is then created. It is like a powerful magnet attracting all kinds of lower vibrational spirit, energy, or entity, and even sometimes people. These entities can then draw off the energy, feed on it, and use it to manifest.

Bodmin Jail (Cornwall) is a place where two such energy lines cross, and therefore they form lower energy vortexes and this, in turn, will also affect the way people behave in such places. They will be prone or influenced to lower vibrational thoughts, paranoia, anger, ego, and fear etc…It can be a source of food to an entity to recharge their essence.

This is a fascinating theory, and if correct, it may go some way toward explaining how the paranormal activity taking place at Bodmin Jail is powered.

Mark offers to show us the path of one of the ley lines. Taking out a pair of dowsing rods, he uses them to map his way from the break room, along the corridor that runs alongside it, to a room at the far end of the hallway on the left. We follow in his footsteps, watching the tips of the rods as they seem to lead him unerringly toward the center of the room.

"I use this room for our glass divination sessions," Kirsten tells us. "There is a very powerful energy source here." Later during the course of our investigation, we will conduct a glass divination exercise of our own in that same room, and end up with some very unexpected results.

"I think that some of the reason behind this haunting is the fact that a number of the inmates should never have been executed for their crimes," Kirsten adds.

"Because they were innocent?" I ask, raising an

eyebrow. She shakes her head.

"No. Because of how trivial those crimes were."

I have to admit that Kirsten has a point. I'm thinking back to the half-hour I spent wandering around the jail the night before, when I had stopped to read some of the informational placards that were posted all about the place. The list of crimes for which someone could be executed made you want to scratch your head and wonder just what the hell the courts of the time had been thinking.

As I've already mentioned, convicts were hanged at Bodmin Jail for such relatively minor crimes as petty theft, highway robbery, forgery, burglary, and arson — crimes that today we would consider serious enough for imprisonment, in most cases, but certainly not execution.

It doesn't take much effort to imagine the resentment, frustration, and even the sheer rage that would arise if you were to receive the death sentence for something so trivial as stealing a sheep or setting fire to a haystack, as some of the prisoners did. Perhaps some of that intense negative emotion found a way to seep into the stone and brickwork of the prison; certainly, some of it still lingers at Bodmin Jail today, if one believes the host of eyewitness accounts of ghostly phenomena that are reported on an almost daily basis.

"Although some of the bodies of the executed men were claimed by their families, quite a few were buried here in the grounds of the jail," Mark says. "That ground wasn't consecrated."

"Wow." Stephen shakes his head sadly. As a man of the cloth, he finds the very idea to be deeply disturbing.

"I think that when the jail first opened, the mentality of British society at the time was that once you were here, you were *here,"* Kirstin opines. "The prison system basically owned you in both life and in death if you were sentenced to be hanged. Some of the spirits may well have continued to have that same belief once they had passed away. Even if you weren't religious, there must still be some comfort to be had from receiving a proper Christian burial. Not all of the executed prisoners — or even those that died of natural causes — would have been granted that final, peaceful gesture.

"It may well be that they're still here inside the jail, because they don't know that they *can* leave…they may not know how to go about leaving. That prisoner mindset could still be holding them captive here."

With the mediumistic abilities that she claims to have,

Kirsten likes to tell any spirit that she encounters within the walls of Bodmin Jail that they are no longer being judged for the crimes that they committed when they were still living.

"Some of these spirits are very forward-thinking and progressive," she continues, gesturing with her hands for emphasis. "They are not all stuck in that prisoner mentality. Some of them really like to listen intently to Mark and I, and also to the other staff members and visitors to the jail. They have a surprisingly good grasp of their situation."

"This is how it is with psychic mediumship," Stephen chimes in. "It's not about verbal communication at all — it's all about thought-forms."

Kirsten nods her head in agreement. "Absolutely. Whenever I'm communicating with the spirits around the jail — or anywhere else, for that matter — they're basically reading my mind. Telepathy is a wonderful gift to have. Whenever we do glass divination, for example, the glass moves in response to the question the split second that I *think* it — not when the words come out of my mouth."

"I've seen that happen a lot," Mark confirms. "Whenever we're doing glass work with visitors here, quite often the glass will move and give the answer to a question that hasn't even been asked yet...and it's usually the *right* answer as well."

I make a mental note of that. Mark and Kirsten are making a fairly bold claim, and I look forward to testing it out for myself later on in our investigation.

We're standing at the top of the second-floor staircase, listening to Mark wax lyrical about some of the jail's lesser-known inmates, when the walkie-talkie he wears at his hip suddenly crackles to life.

"Where are you?" It's Kirsten. A minute or two later she appears, accompanied by a middle-aged gentleman in a very smart suit. He greets us warmly, and asks what we're doing at the jail. Both Mark and Kirsten seem more than a little deferential to him, and I'm getting a 'this is the boss' vibe. My hunch turns out to be correct. His name is Vince, and he represents the ownership of the jail. Fortunately for us, he's nice and polite, and only has glowing things to say about the place and its employees.

"Are you lot paranormal people?" Vince asks. When we nod, he lets out a theatrical *"Oooooh!"* as if to indicate that the ghostly side of things isn't really his cup of tea. Vince has a broad London-area accent. He's very affectionate toward the jail though, and I find myself warming to him almost instantly. I like his matter-of-fact style, which seems totally down to Earth and up-front.

Vince recounts the story of how he first got involved with Bodmin Jail. His employers bought the place and asked him if he wanted to be involved with the restoration project. Not entirely sure, Vince came down to Cornwall to see the place for himself. "As soon as I walked in for the first time, I started to get the feeling that somebody was telling me, *'bring us back,'*" he recalls. "'Make some *life* in this building.' That's when I decided that I was happy to get involved."

We all wander casually from cell to cell, and I make a point of standing behind Vince and watching him. It's a habit that all paramedics have. We're constantly watching people, observing their little habits and mannerisms. It tends to make us skilled at picking out liars and bullshit artists. Everything about Vince's manner convinces me that he's telling us the truth, and I'm glad that our paths have crossed.

"The paranormal frightens the life out of me," he chuckles. We all join in with the laughter. Almost perfectly timed, a low rumble comes from somewhere over our heads:

the sound of thunder. It's only then that we realize that a thunderstorm has crept in. Lesley tries to nip outside for a crafty cigarette, and despite her heavy overcoat, comes back in looking as bedraggled as a drowned rat.

"Oh dear," I deadpan, watching a single raindrop plip from the end of her nose. "Is it raining outside?" She answers me with two fingers, and not in the manner of Winston Churchill, either.

I'd initially thought that having met us and making some polite small-talk for a while, Vince would have taken his leave and headed home. Instead, he sticks with us for a bit longer and asks Kirsten and Mark if they've taken us to the Naval Prison yet.

"We're not allowed to," Kirsten reminds him gently. "It's off-limits to all visitors, remember? Because of the construction."

"Not to me, it bloody well isn't!" Vince booms, suddenly animated. He's now a man on a mission. Leaning toward me, he says, "What do you think, paranormal fella? Do you want to go on a little field trip?"

I don't even have to think about it. "Oh, *HELL YES!*" Stephen and Lesley are just as excited. We'd been told that there was no possibility of us ever getting to investigate that part of the jail, and now our savior had arrived in the rather unlikely form of a dapper businessman from London. This has to be the finest example of synchronicity I've experienced in a long time. Eagerly, we gather up some basic equipment — voice recorders and Stephen's Spirit Box — and head for the exit. Hopefully our gear will survive the downpour.

Kirsten goes first and immediately regrets it. The heavy steel door is flung open by the wind. A wall of torrential rain hits her full-on in the face. Undeterred, she hands the door off to Mark and heads out into the night. We all follow in a single line, one after the other. The rain is sheeting down on us from above and all sides, soaking through our jackets and trousers, but we're as giddy as a bunch of schoolchildren going on holiday.

Following the long wall around the side of the main jail building, Kirsten and Mark lead us toward the looming stone structure of the former Naval Prison. The years have not been kind to this grand old building. Broken stones look like jagged teeth, silhouetted against the grey night sky. Every few minutes we get another loud boom, though at least there's precious little lightning. I can't speak for my companions, but I have absolutely no desire to meet my maker after being struck by a bolt of lightning in the middle of a haunted prison. Call me old-fashioned, if you will.

We splash our way through streams of rainwater running downhill, trying our best to avoid the deeper puddles — at least, most of us do. Vince, whose smartly-polished shoes look like they cost more than my entire wardrobe, doesn't hesitate for a second. His suit is already drenched, but the man doesn't seem to care a jot. He's so enthusiastic to show us the Naval Prison, he catches up with Mark and Kirsten before they even make it to the locked gate in the construction fence. We all gather around him, shoulders hunched into our coats and our electrical equipment tucked deep into our pockets, while Vince makes an announcement.

"This is completely out of bounds," he tells us, raising his voice to be heard over the downpour. "Now, *I'm* happy to proceed, but we're not going in unless *you're* all totally happy to, okay?"

"We're 'appy!" Lesley says. We all nod enthusiastically, keen to get in out of the rain but even more excited about getting into the jail's one forbidden area.

"In other words, if anything falls on your head and kills you, don't come back and sue me," Kirsten smiles.

"Well, *I'll* definitely come back," I tell her, "but I don't exactly have a ghost lawyer, so you don't need to worry about that."

All jokes aside, Stephen, Lesley and I all appreciate what a big deal this is. Vince is going out on a limb for us, a potential health and safety nightmare if anybody gets hurt. But he's determined to let us experience this part of the jail for ourselves, and I am grateful beyond words to be given the opportunity. No matter what happens in there, if somebody falls and breaks a leg (or worse, their neck) we're all going into this with our eyes wide open. Nobody is going to sue if things go awry. All three of us give our word, which is good enough for Vince. He pops the padlock with a key and swings the gate open.

And just like that, we're inside the Naval Prison and the ruins of the nearby Civil Wing, which branches off from it at an angle.

Mud splatters up around our ankles. We duck in out of the rain, which is easier said than done because the roof is long gone, and much of this wing is open to the frigid night air. I've seen the architect's drawings of what the Naval Prison and the Civil Wing are going to look like, once the restoration is complete, but right now it looks like the sort of place that horror movies are filmed in.

Vince shows us where the separate male and female sections of the Civil Wing are. I imagine that under normal circumstances, the acoustics are incredible in here, but tonight all sounds are muffled by the rain. Still, the atmosphere has to be felt to be believed. There's a heaviness that is difficult to put into words, pervading the entire wing. The structure is crumbling, with what once would have been sections of interior staircases fully exposed and jutting out into thin air. It's nothing less than magnificent to behold, the kind of decaying wonder that people like us really appreciate.

"Wow," Stephen whispers, shaking his head in amazement. If I'm picking up on a strange atmosphere, I can only imagine what *he's* feeling with his special sensitivities. I watch him walk through the shadows, following his instincts toward where the energies feel strongest.

We gather together in one of the old cells on the ground level (there's no way we'd dare climb any higher, or the entire building might come crashing down around our ears). By mutual agreement, all of our flashlights are switched off. Everybody just stands there quietly, soaking in the ambience. The sound of raindrops pitter-pattering on stone makes it an almost mystical experience for us. I may be deluding myself, but it feels as if I'm already starting to make a deep connection with those souls who once inhabited this wing of the jail.

It suddenly strikes me that it's the middle of the night, in the middle of a storm, and I'm standing in a forbidden part of a historic, haunted jail with some of the most wonderful people I've ever met. Life just doesn't get any better than this, and I take a minute or two just to savor the moment, to really experience it fully. At the back of my mind, I know that I'll end up trying to describe it to my readers in the future, and there's no way my words will be adequate to the task.

"This place *does* speak to you," Stephen says after a while. "It's not dead at all. Far from it." He rests a hand on a cold, stone fireplace, something that hasn't seen an actual flame in over a hundred years. Closing his eyes, he lets out a long, contented sigh. From the sound of it, there's nowhere else in the world he'd rather be.

I know exactly how he feels.

The priest opens his eyes again. "Let's try a burst EVP session," he suggests, taking out his audio recorder and setting it down on the closest flat surface that's out of the rain.

"This place is absolutely amazing," Stephen begins. "Would you like to talk to us? To *any* of us?"

"Are you happy with the work that's being done here," Lesley wants to know.

"Are you excited that the building is coming back to life?" It's Stephen again.

I ask whether this place is home to them.

All we can here are the raindrops spattering on the stonework and the muffled sound of cars in the distance.

"Were you happy in this place?" I ask, and then change my tense. "*Are* you happy in this place?"

More questions follow. Where are the potential communicators from — Cornwall, or somewhere further afield? Is there any message that they would like to convey?

The session lasts a smidgen over three minutes. We don't review the audio on the spot — it's far too noisy, and we're all soaked to the bone. Besides, our time in this part of the jail is very limited, and I don't want us to drag our feet. Evidence review can wait until later.

The group follows Mark from the Civil Wing into the former Naval Prison, which looks very similar to it in the darkness. He's using a flashlight to guide us on our way, and miraculously, nobody slips, trips, or slides into the muck.

We run another three-minute burst session using very similar questions, just for the sake of consistency, and then Stephen fires up the Spirit Box he's been lugging around under his coat. Static blares from the device's single speaker, its hissing echo bouncing from the walls of our newly-chosen cell. This small space would once have been occupied by a member of the Royal Navy, sentenced to time in the 'glass house' for some infraction or other. Now it's home to a bunch of very cold, wet, but still thoroughly excited paranormal investigators.

Once again, Stephen leads off with the questioning. Rather than participate, I'm content to simply stand back and watch this time. Although our burst EVP sessions ultimately won't turn out to yield anything of significance, the Spirit Box session does: we capture fragments of voices, which is nothing particularly unusual for a device that is basically a variable-sweep radio scanner — except for the fact that these voices, all of them male, are speaking in a language other than English.

The phrases are short and to the point, but undeniably German. There are some *jas*, *neins*, and *bittes*. There's even one *danke schoen*. Another word borders on the obscene. We find this pretty impressive. Many skeptics believe that the so-called Spirit Box is a useless device, fooling the listener into believing that random word fragments or bursts of static are actually meaningful words and phrases. "You're just picking up radio programs, DJs chattering, and that sort of thing," is a common refrain. While that is definitely true sometimes, it most certainly doesn't account for what we hear in the Naval Prison during this particular session. For starters, how would *German* voices be speaking over the airwaves? No German radio stations broadcast as far as the south coast of England, and even assuming that they did, then why don't we pick up German voices anywhere else in the jail? They only emerge when we are experimenting in the wing which had once housed German Prisoners of War. If that's not paranormal, then it seems like quite the coincidence.

After about ten minutes have passed, the voices stop speaking. In unspoken agreement, we make our way back to the main jail. Nobody wants to push our luck and give the impression of taking advantage of Vince's largesse. Thanking him for his willingness to bend the rules for us, we bid farewell to Vince and head back inside to warm up. Our teeth are chattering and we're all shivering. I've never been so grateful to accept a cup of tea from Lesley in my entire life.

Showing uncharacteristically poor judgment, Stephen takes a seat in the hallway outside the break room, unaware that he's parked himself a little too close to the electric heater. Before he realizes what's going on, we can all smell the distinctive odor of singed priest. Steam is rising from the back of his sopping wet trousers, but he's only just starting to feel the scorch marks on the back of his legs.

"Yikes!" He jumps up out of the chair like a rocket taking off. The rest of us crack up. I'm laughing so hard that I almost spill my tea. Rubbing his sore backside, Stephen laughs himself despite having come perilously close to inadvertently setting himself on fire.

"Now I have sympathy for the victims of the Spanish Inquisition," he mutters, reaching out for a cookie and munching on it.

"You've got to admit, it would have made one hell of a headline," I laugh. "Priest spontaneously combusts at Bodmin Jail. Our breaking news at ten."

Along with the hot tea, the unexpected hilarity has helped to warm us all up.

"So, what's next, then?" Lesley asks. Kirsten and Mark raise their eyebrows as if to say, *We can go wherever you want to go*. Poking my head outside, I verify that the rain has stopped. I don't know how long this break in the bad weather will last for, so it seems wise to make good use of it.

"What about the hanging pit?"

"You what?" Lesley looks at me as though I've grown a second head. "What do you want to go down there for?"

"Because it's a *hanging pit*, Lesley, and when do you get the chance to investigate one of those?"

"Yeah, I suppose," she concedes. "Good point."

CHAPTER TEN
The Hanging Pit

Kirsten unlocks the exterior door and opens it. Thankfully, the rain has tapered off to little more than a light drizzle. We make our way along the side of the jail and out into the courtyard. The execution shed is off to our left. Ducking underneath the dangling noose, Mark opens up the heavy wooden doors that cover the pit and throws them both aside. A rickety-looking staircase-cum-ladder leads down into the blackness at the bottom of the pit. It looks steeper than the house prices in London, but there's no backing out now. One by one, we each climb slowly down into the pit. Halfway down the steps, I have Stephen carefully hand me his Spirit Box.

Just as one might expect, the floor of the pit is full of water, deep enough that it comes up to the level of our shoes. There are also hidden patches of sucking mud lurking just below the waterline, which we all try our best to avoid, but it's easier said than done. When the last person has climbed down, everything is eerily quiet. The brick walls make our own voices echo back at us, and when nobody's speaking, all we can hear is the sound of five people collectively breathing in an enclosed space.

It's dark down here in the pit. Looking up, I see the noose swaying gently back and forth some ten or twelve feet above my head, contrasting starkly against the brooding grey sky. Unbidden, my imagination kicks into high gear. I'm suddenly picturing the body of a man swinging to and fro, left to hang for the regulation one hour before being brought down and formally pronounced dead. A shudder runs through me that has nothing to do with the cold or my still-damp clothes. Handing Stephen his Spirit Box, I give myself a hug in a vain attempt to stop the shivering.

"I'm feeling a great sense of disappointment down here," Kirsten says, looking around as her eyes adjust to the darkness. Beyond that, she isn't willing to be drawn.

An ethereal voice suddenly fills the pit, accompanied by a string of colorful L.E.D. lights. Stephen has fired up his Spirit Box, and the usual stream of nonsensical noise is reverberating from the walls.

From between chattering teeth, we each take turns asking questions. All that comes back by way of reply is complete gibberish – until Kirsten steps up.

"Were men or women hanged here?" she asks, fully aware that only men were executed in the hanging pit.

Never hanged here, the box says.

Kirsten suddenly steps back, scraping up against the wall behind her. We all turn to look at her quizzically. "Somebody just took hold of my arm," she explains. Lesley shines a flashlight over in her direction. Although we're all huddled relatively close together, nobody is physically touching Kirsten. "I can still feel it. As if somebody is holding me here." She indicates her bicep with the other hand.

Next, it's Lesley's turn to be startled. "Something just touched the back of my legs," she insists, recoiling. There's nothing behind her but the smooth brick of the pit, and Lesley's certain she didn't simply brush against it.

Somebody's here, says the Spirit Box, in what seems like a very sinister way. Several other voices chime in, drowning this speaker out.

"Ooof!" Lesley is suddenly shoved from behind. She throws out her arms to stop herself from falling face-first into the filth. "I just got pushed!"

"Are you sure you didn't just stumble?" I ask, ever the skeptic

"Yes, I'm sure," she insists, shooting me what I'm sure is a dirty look. "It was a proper push from the back."

Kirsten tells us that she is being touched in the small of her back now. She then adds that whatever invisible watcher is down here with us in the hanging pit, she's sensing that they're *very* interested in us and what we're doing here.

Suddenly, the back of my neck feels *freezing* — ice cold. All of the hairs are standing on end, just like the old cliche goes. But there's no breeze behind me; the only thing back there is a solid brick wall. Just as suddenly as the feeling came on, it disappears again, leaving me totally nonplussed.

"Do you want us to leave?" Lesley asks. For ten seconds, nothing intelligible comes through the box in answer to her question. Then, a female voice, one that we haven't heard before, distinctly says the word *UP!*

The implication here is obvious. *Something* wants us up and out of here. The water is also beginning to slowly rise up, lapping around our ankles now; it's probably just the runoff from elsewhere in the prison leaking through into the hanging pit. We've been down here for a good fifteen minutes, and it seems like an appropriate time to take our leave.

One by one, we clamber back up the rickety staircase, passing Stephen's Spirit Box up and setting it on the lip of the pit. When the last person has come up, Mark carefully closes the doors again. I can't help but wonder if our invisible toucher has come back up with us.

I'm done, says the Spirit Box. And just like that, it is. Nothing more than random noises come through it over the course of the next few minutes. Finally, Stephen switches the device off. "I think they might need a break," he says, tucking it under one arm and starting off for the main jail. "I know that *I* do."

"Is there a cup of tea in my future, Lesley?" I ask.

"Maybe," she smiles cheerfully, apparently over her annoyance already. "*If* you're a good boy."

Following the obligatory tea break, we head back outside to investigate the former medical building, which stands directly opposite the execution shed. When Mark lets us inside, I notice two things. One, that the structure is deceptively large on the inside (rather like Bodmin Jail's answer to *Dr. Who's* TARDIS) and two, that it appears to be used mostly for junk storage. The atmosphere inside feels very flat, even to somebody with my extremely limited sensitivities. Nevertheless, we spend half an hour conducting

EVP burst sessions and attempting to communicate with anybody that might be willing to talk to us.

No such luck.

Still, as every paranormal investigator knows, you win some, you lose some. It's impossible to get good results in every part of a location, and the medical building seems to be inert tonight. We return to the jail and Stephen announces that he's sensing very strong energies at the far end of the ground floor hallway which branches off from the break room.

That's going to be our next target.

CHAPTER ELEVEN
Glassed

Sunrise isn't far away, and we have just enough time left for one more experiment before packing our bags and heading back to the Jamaica Inn for the final time on this trip. Mark and Kirsten suggest that we try some glass work in one of the more active rooms at the end of the corridor, the same one in which Stephen was picking up 'very strong energies.'

Stephen and Lesley have never given glass work a try before, but I'm familiar with it, having used the technique with some success at the Clink prison in Southwark, London. It is a method of purported spirit communication that dates back at least as far as the Victorian era, and can sometimes yield results that border on the downright spectacular. The glass can take on a life of its own, whizzing around the table at great speed, much to the amazement and mystification of those who are taking part.

As with most methods for attempting to contact spirit entities, glass work (or glass *divination,* as some prefer to call it) is extremely simple. All that is needed is a firm, smooth surface, usually a table or something similar, and an ordinary glass. Nothing mystical or particularly exotic is required. Kirsten kindly supplies us with a plain old wine glass and a sturdy wooden table that's about two feet in diameter.

The idea is that each participant places the tip of one finger lightly on top of the glass. A non-participating observer then calls out to any beings that might be present and offers them the opportunity to use the glass in order to communicate.

"We used to do this all the time when I was a boy," Mark explains as Kirsten carefully positions the table and glass to her satisfaction in the center of the room. "Whenever there was a power cut, my aunt would lay out a table in front of the fireplace, she'd put an upside-down wine glass on it, and we'd talk to the dead relatives until the lights came back on. We did it by candle-light and it worked every time."

Despite its simplicity, glass divination is a controversial technique. Skeptics will usually argue that the glass moves because the participants are inadvertently pushing it themselves. I think that there is some merit to this argument, though I don't believe that conscious fraud is involved. Pretty much everybody who takes place in a paranormal investigation or 'ghost hunt' is there to try and gather evidence of life after death in some way, shape, or form;

when the night goes by without any such evidence being gathered, it can often be enormously disappointing. Nobody likes to have their time wasted, after all, and practically all of us have a deep, subconscious desire to please, to not let down the social group we are currently with.

It is therefore believed to be a series of tiny subconscious micro-muscular movements known as the *ideomotor reflex* that cause the glass to move, opponents of glass divination state, rather than any sort of discarnate entity such as a spirit being. The participants are not doing this deliberately, for the most part, and generally aren't even aware that they are influencing the movements of the glass at all. This is believed to be the same mechanism behind other techniques for spirit communication such as the Ouija Board and the so-called 'Human Pendulum.'

With that being said, I am not convinced that the ideomotor reflex can necessarily account for *all* such instances. I have kept my finger resting so lightly on top of the glass that it was barely making contact with its surface at all, even wanting to slip off every time the glass moved. However, a healthy streak of skepticism should be a part of every good paranormal investigator's tool-kit, so I decide to throw in one or two control measures during our session in an attempt to find out whether the innate suggestibility of the participants was behind it all…or if some other power is at work.

I don't let anybody know my plans in advance. To be clear, my own personal position on glasswork is one of uncertainty — I simply *don't know* whether we are communicating with spirits, our own subconscious minds, or whether something else is at play entirely. All that I can say for sure is that I will continue to use this method for as long as it yields interesting results; if those results can be cross-checked by some other means, providing more tangible, objective results, then so much the better.

"We use this table expressly for glass work and nothing else," Mark tells us, "and we only ever do it in this room, which is on the north-east corner of the jail. A ley line runs directly underneath here and provides a lot of energy."

To illustrate his point, he uses a pair of dowsing rods to indicate the path of the ley line, just as he had done before. Again, it seems to terminate at a point just beyond the center of the room.

Stephen, Lesley and I take up positions around the table, each resting a fingertip on the base of the glass. Mark leaves the room, explaining that for some reason the technique never seems to work when he is present. He switches off the light on his way out and goes off for a well-earned cup of tea and a biscuit.

Kirsten asks us to focus all of our energy upon the glass, which we duly attempt to do. We're working in conditions of semi-darkness, with only the light from the corridor outside to see by.

"I can feel it wanting to move already," Lesley whispers.

"If there are any spirits from the jail that want to talk to us, please step into this room now and communicate," Kirsten calls out. "Then use the energy of the people around the table to move the glass. You can also use *my* energy, if you wish."

No sooner has Kirsten finished speaking than we feel the glass begin to move under our fingers. The three of us exchange the obligatory "Is that you moving the glass?" looks, then shake our heads to indicate that none of us is…not consciously, at least.

The glass starts out by making a lazy clockwise circle, its lip scraping on the wooden tabletop. Before long, it begins to pick up speed, moving faster and faster until it it's practically whizzing around, then starts to fall inward as it transitions into describing a spiral shape. The inward spiral suddenly reverses itself, and soon the glass is circling again. Kirsten entreats whatever spirit is controlling the glass to move it faster — "*much* faster, please, spirit" — and it dutifully obeys, picking up the pace until the three of us can barely rest our hands on top of the glass. She then asks it to stop and move to the center of the table. It obeys. Stephen, Lesley, and I readjust the position of our fingertips, which are beginning to sweat ever so slightly and slip off the glass.

"Can you please bring the glass to me, so that we all know that *you* know where I am in the room?" Kirsten asks. Obediently, the glass shoots directly toward her. "Thank you. Could you now move the glass to one of the men on this table?" The glass moves backward to sit in front of Stephen. When Kirsten asks it to locate the other man at the table, I'm praying that it will go toward Lesley, purely for the comedic value, but instead it comes straight toward me. After that, when asked whether there is a lady standing at the table, the glass identifies Lesley straight away.

Using the movements of the glass to answer, Kirsten begins to ask a series of yes/no questions. Was the spirit connected to Bodmin Jail? *Yes*, or so it claims to be. While that might seem like an obvious thing to ask, it's equally possible that one of the investigators present (including

Mark, who is back in the break room, keeping watch over us via the video camera feed) could have brought a spirit attachment along with us. It happens more often than one might think.

Whatever is moving the glass tells us that it had also been with us in a different part of the jail earlier tonight. We subsequently narrow this location down to being the Naval Prison, the place in which the five of us had huddled together in the abandoned cells while trying to keep the rain off.

The entity claims to have been a young Cornish boy, and is supposedly standing just off to Kirsten's left side. The boy, who is described as being about seven years old and possessing a club foot, says that he had tried to speak with us back in the prison cells but had been unable to. Kirsten asks him whether he is happy and feeling well today. The response might best be described as indifferent or sluggish, and remains so when she enquires whether the spirit is aware that the weather is foul tonight.

Apparently, the dead boy had been resident in the Naval Prison for quite a long time. Another spirit also accompanied him, a lady who would not have been permitted to spend time with him when they were both incarcerated in the jail.

We're told by the glass that the woman was, in fact, the boy's mother. Back in the days when Bodmin Jail was still a functioning prison, it wasn't unusual for children to end up there, especially if there was nobody else to take care of them on the outside.

Kirsten breaks off for a moment, saying that she has just heard a voice. She asks the glass whether it was the spirit entity speaking to her. The glass slides over to YES. Unfortunately, this is a completely subjective event, because when we check, the voice is not picked up on any of our audio recorders. More's the pity.

"Would your mother like to talk to us?" Kirsten asks. The boy's mother seems to be willing, as the glass immediately picks up speed again, tearing around the table like a crazed dervish. Our hostess frowns. "I'm sensing that she's not quite as happy as her son. Could you take the glass to where you're standing, please?"

The glass crosses the board and makes a bee line toward Kirsten's right hand side, the opposite side to where the boy was supposed to be. At her prompting, we all greet the female spirit (feeling just a little bit strange about speaking to an invisible somebody) and we immediately notice a definite change in the feeling of the glass beneath our fingertips. The motion seems to drag more, to be a little heavier and more sluggish. Gone is the boyish exuberance with which it had flashed around the table at the beginning of the session. Maybe it's just our collective imagination, but now it seems almost as if there is a certain reluctance to its movements, one that hadn't been there just a few moments before.

Kirsten adds that she had seen the form of a woman accompanying us on our return trip from the old Naval Prison, although she hadn't noticed the figure of a young boy at the time. She describes a female figure of slender build, wearing a long dress, one that required her to lift the hem of it up in order to prevent it from getting soaked in one of the many puddles that we had been splashing through. I find it intriguing that while the young boy said that he was unaware of the weather conditions, the spirit who claimed to be his mother appeared to be fully cognizant of them.

"Are you also aware of the condition of the building — did you know they're going to put the roof back on? We'll be able to see our beautiful roof again…" The glass goes bananas, almost jerking itself away from my fingertip. I can't help but wonder whether the nameless woman approves of the restoration plans or not. When one considers the fact that it really was the only way to save Bodmin Jail and keep it running, her opinion — and mine, for that matter — is really beside the point.

Further questioning reveals that this particular lady had suffered some sort of ailment with her leg, one that required her to be treated in the medical building for a short time. Kirsten then gives us the opportunity to ask our own questions.

This is the point at which I want to throw some of my own test questions into the mix. As interesting as the glass session has been so far, we have to consider the possibility that Kirsten is either delusional or simply making it all up. While that might sound rude, it certainly isn't meant to be; viewing things from a skeptical point of view is essential when one is testing extraordinary claims. Having spent the past two nights working with her, I find Kirsten to be credible, and have no reason to doubt her integrity, but I would be delinquent if I didn't consider all of the possible angles.

"I'd like to please ask you, spirit, how many fingers am I holding up?" Before asking the question, I surreptitiously place my left hand behind my back, keeping the right hand in position so that my pointer finger is still resting on the base of the wine glass. I've taken great care to make sure that neither Stephen, Lesley, or Kirsten can see my hand, angling my torso in just such a way as to mask it from them all. "Am I holding up one finger?"

The glass fails to move.

"Am I holding up two fingers?" Nothing. "Am I holding up three?"

Still nothing. I keep my tone carefully neutral, making sure that I don't place any undue emphasis on the words *one, two, three,* or *four,* so that I won't unwittingly give away the right answer.

"Am I holding up four fingers?"

The glass suddenly springs to life, dashing across the board in a clockwise circle. I bring my hand out with a flourish to show everybody my four straight fingers. Understandably, Kirsten seems to feel vindicated. I had made absolutely sure not to exert even the slightest pressure upon the glass at any point, and even if my fellow investigators have been influencing it somehow, they would only have had a twenty percent or one-in-five chance of guessing the correct number — not exactly the greatest of odds in their favor.

"This is quite a severe, straight-faced lady." Kirsten

begins to describe the spirit entity who she says is manipulating the glass. "She's rather sullen in nature and doesn't find things very amusing. Her attitude is basically, 'What was the point in that?'"

I decide that it might be best for me to try and explain the purpose of my quick little experiment, just so that there are no misunderstandings.

"Thank you for being gracious enough to cooperate with me on that," I begin. "I wanted to test to see whether you were a figment of our imagination, or whether you are truly, objectively real. Does that make any sense to you?"

The glass makes a slow, lazy circle. I'm guessing that the answer is a somewhat disapproving *yes*.

Now it's Stephen's turn. He clears his throat. "So…are you really free of pain?"

Nothing happens for a moment. "You may have to define which type of pain you're talking about," Kirsten interjects. "Physical, mental, emotional…there are many types."

"Physical pain," the priest clarifies. The answer is once again *yes*. "What about emotional pain?" The glass immediately halts. Even though she must be far beyond the state of physical suffering, it is still sad to think that this long-dead woman could be suffering some sort of emotional distress.

Stephen asks whether the young lad that is present is the lady's only son, to which the answer is once again *yes*. I ask whether the mysterious woman had died here at Bodmin Jail; she had not, and neither, it turns out, had her son — which begs the question, why would either one of them haunt the jail in the first place?

Kirsten has an answer for that. "They have come back here at the same relative ages as when they were actually here in life. I believe that both of them went on to have long and happy lives. Both of them still have a connection with Bodmin Jail, though, and I don't think it was a particularly unhappy place for them to be. It still isn't. Looking at it from her perspective, this was a better place for her and her son to be than outside. It was warm; it was dry; and it was relatively safe."

Next, I ask whether this lady was innocent of the crime for which she had been convicted. I have to admit that I'm fully expecting the glass to go flying around the table at this point; after all, if you were to ask an inmate of any prison whether they were innocent or not, the odds are good that they would say that they were. As the old saying goes, everybody is innocent in jail. It therefore comes as a surprise to me when the glass stubbornly refuses to budge. Kirsten reports that the female spirit has just said, "I did it."

This refreshing level of honesty rather takes me aback. I conjecture that the crime couldn't have been all that serious, as most major crimes (and far too many minor ones) were punishable by execution at Bodmin Jail. Kirsten is fairly confident that she can guess the nature of the woman's crime, and Lesley is thinking along the very same lines, because she asks whether she had stolen something, to which the glass answers with a laconic scrape across the tabletop.

"Was it out of necessity?" Stephen wants to know. As a holy man, he is always trying to see the best in people — and far too often finds himself disappointed. This turns out to be one of those times. The glass just sits there, practically daring us to judge her. I ask if she had stolen whatever it was out of pure greed, which is immediately confirmed.

Now it's time to play 'guess the stolen item.' In the end, we ascertain that it was neither money or food, but rather a piece of jewelry that had caught the woman's eye, a trinket that had belonged to her former employer.

"She was looking for a relatively safe place to raise her son," Kirsten explains, "So she committed a small crime, one that she knew they wouldn't hang her for."

I ask the spirit whether this was indeed the case. In response, the glass makes several laps of the board. "Stop, please," I tell it. The glass abruptly stops moving.

"Oh, she's just shot you a nasty look," Kirsten says, visibly wincing.

"Why?"

"Because you asked her to stop before she was ready."

"I did say *please,*" I point out. The last thing I want is to get on the bad side of any entity that might be resident at the jail; the consequences of taking that lightly can be very negative, and all too real, as I have learned to my cost in the past. This is why, despite my being an agnostic, I always make a point of asking Stephen to offer up some light and prayer before we leave a haunted location. It's a sincere attempt to keep anything negative or angry from following us back.

Speaking very formally, I say, "Would you be kind enough to forgive me for my impertinence, please?"

The glass springs to life again. Hopefully, my apology has gotten me off the hook…maybe. I guess that only time will tell.

"Am I back in your good graces again?" The glass stops

dead. *Apparently not, then,* I think. Hopefully this won't come back to bite me later on.

"She's a very proud lady, this one, quite haughty," says Kirsten. We all need to remember that when we deal with her from now on.

Attempting to lighten the mood, Lesley asks whether the spirit thinks that I should make her a cup of tea. As our regular gourmet tea-maker, Lesley is trying to pull a fast one. I laugh happily when it appears that the spirit does not endorse her view regarding the tea, for the glass doesn't budge an inch. Looking back, I can't help but think that if the glass work really *was* attributable to our own subconscious pushing, then this would have been the time for Lesley to unwittingly give the glass the tiniest little nudge. Instead, she's crestfallen when instead the spirit seems to take my side.

"Oh, I *like* her," I grin. Yet my assumption that the spirit is on Team Richard proves to be false, as Kirsten is about to make clear.

"Tea is a rarity for this woman. It would have been a very rare — for her, anyway — and precious treat. Her attitude is like, *Oh, there's tea?!?"* She affects a look of wide-eyed wonder.

Seizing my chance, I ask whether the lady would like me to have Lesley step away and make her a cup of tea. The answer is a most enthusiastic *yes*. "Karma can be *very* quick sometimes, can't it, Lesley?" I smirk. She glares daggers across the table at me.

With a little further questioning, Kirsten coaxes out of the woman that making tea was perceived to be a woman's task back in her day, and not the sort of thing that most men would bother with. That makes sense to us, for such sexism was a social norm during the nineteenth century.

It dawns on me that I have been suddenly presented with an unexpected opportunity to score some points with this former inmate of the jail. "Madame, after all these years, would you like it if a man finally made some tea and brought it for you as an offering?"

That really seems to grab her attention. The glass goes ballistic. Kirsten tells us that the lady is both embarrassed and quite taken aback by my offer. She seems flattered that a man would make tea for her, but also worried that it might be some sort of trap that I had set. I reassure her that it is nothing of the kind, and then step away from the table, leaving Stephen and Lesley as the only active participants.

"I will bring you a very special cup of tea, one made *just* for you," I promise. This earns the most energetic glass response of the night — in fact, it looks as if the glass is going to fly off the table and shatter on the ground, so great is its momentum. Stephen and Lesley have a hard time keeping their fingers in contact without exerting any pressure on its base.

I wander off back to the break room, where Mark is hanging out and watching the screens. We chat for a while as I make a cup of tea for the phantom lady, choosing what I hope will be perceived as being the poshest, most exotic available: a lemon-flavored blend. The investigators call out that they would like a cup of hot chocolate for the spirit of the young boy, which Mark quickly drums up and hands to me.

The spirit's excitement doesn't seem to have diminished in the slightest by the time I get back. The glass is still moving around the table in a very lively manner, despite the fact that there are now only two remaining participants giving it energy. When I come back into the room, Kirsten is telling Stephen and Lesley that the ghostly little boy is now holding onto his mother's hand, an image that we all find to be rather endearing.

I set the cup of hot chocolate down carefully on one side

of the table, and place the tea-cup down on the other. Once again, the glass shoots off at high speed. Kirsten tells us that the lady has just sent her son across to the opposite side of the room, and then asks her whether it is acceptable for me to rejoin the participants on the glass, which it apparently is. She then goes on to enquire where exactly the female spirit wants me to stand. Without hesitation, the glass indicates a spot next to where the woman is said to be standing.

"Wow!" Kirsten exclaims, obviously impressed. "This is nothing short of *amazing,* the fact that she's willing to let you stand next to her. Think about it from her point of view. She comes from a time that is much more formal and restrictive than our own. She is a single woman with a child, after all. I get the impression that she normally wouldn't behave like this, but she is *very* happy that you made her tea…"

"Well, it's the little things in life that count," I say awkwardly, ever so slightly embarrassed.

"That may also be why she just sent her little boy to the other side of the room," she adds, adopting a slightly mischievous tone, "because she would usually never want to be seen standing this close to a man when her son could see it."

I look at Stephen and Lesley in turn, and could swear that they are both fighting to hold back a smirk. To be fair, it's hard to blame them. This is the first time in my life that I have ever, to all intents and purposes, *flirted* with a ghost. To tell the truth, it's also more than a little surreal.

Kirsten tells the female spirit that Stephen and I have come all the way from America, and points out that it is possible for her to connect with either of us if she chooses to do so, no matter how much distance lies between Cornwall and our homes in Colorado. Stephen and I both tell the spirit of the lady that she is more than welcome to drop by from time to time for a visit…but emphasize that she isn't permitted to follow us back or take up residence with us. After all, I'd have one hell of a time explaining *that* to my wife…

Stephen is curious. "Can you truly connect with the living over long distances and visit them anywhere you want to?" According to the motion of the glass, yes, she can. Unable to stop myself, I ask the lady politely if she would be kind enough to leave me some kind of unmistakable sign that she had dropped by my house, in order to say hello.

"I've just seen what she is planning to do," Kirsten says, "and there's no way you're going to miss a sign like this. I'll write it down on a piece of paper, seal it in an envelope, and give it to Mark. I think you're going to have quite the reaction when it happens, that's all I'm going to say at the moment."

Thinking that it sounds more than a little ominous, I nevertheless agree. *After all,* I tell myself, *what's the worst that could happen...?*

"We have to go now," Lesley says, sounding genuinely sad. None of us really wants to leave. Our in-depth investigation of Bodmin Jail has been so fascinating, and all of us feel that there is so much more to uncover here. It practically mandates a return visit at some point in the future. The old place has barely begun to give up its secrets to us yet.

"Don't worry, you will be back here at some point," Kirsten tells us. She sounds absolutely convinced of it, and I find myself hoping that she is right about that. Bodmin Jail has some kind of pull, indefinable but at the same time very strong. I already want to spend more time here, which may seem a little odd when one considers just what exactly has happened to people inside these prison walls over the years. It is, nonetheless, a very tangible sensation, and one that I'm not inclined to resist.

The three of us say our goodbyes to the spirit of the lady and her little boy, and then follow Kirsten back to the main room. Under my breath, I ask her how long it will probably take for the woman to pay a visit to my home. She replies that I will most likely get the sign that I had been promised within the space of a month.

We talk about the spirit of the lady and her son for a few minutes longer. "Making the tea for her was a huge deal. It made her feel like absolute royalty," Kirsten explains to me. "When you were out of the room, Richard, I could see her preening herself. She wanted to tidy herself up a little bit while you were gone and make sure that she was presenting herself at her very best. The tea won her over. If you hadn't made it for her, I am convinced that she wouldn't have been nearly as responsive to you as that."

I can't help but think that the spirit's concern for her appearance was just a little bit wasted on me, considering that I couldn't actually see her at all.

"Ooooh," Stephen chuckles, nudging me in the ribs. "Your wife had better watch out…"

"Oh, shut up, priest." I'm glad that none of them can see me blushing in the low light.

"Well, if nothing else, I got to finally see you make a

cup of tea," Lesley says, laughing happily. "Never mind all the ghosts, that was worth the trip all by itself."

Lesley, Stephen and I thank Mark and Kirsten for the many hours of time they have kindly spent with us. It is still dark outside, and freezing cold, but it won't be long until sunrise. As we stand outside the jail waiting for our taxi to arrive, I can't help but look back at this magnificent old building with a sense of great affection. I find myself thinking about its ghosts, not just the phantom lady and her young boy, but also the countless others that are said to still walk its haunted hallways and dwell within its cells and common areas.

Mark locks the heavy front gate behind us, and I catch one last glimpse of the hanging pit before it slams shut. It is a tired and weary trio of paranormal investigators that climb into the taxi this morning, yet we are also elated and feeling very satisfied indeed with our brief period of incarceration at Bodmin Jail. I watch it disappear in the rear-view mirror, quickly getting lost in my own thoughts. Beside me, Stephen is quietly going through his usual post-investigation protective ritual, mouthing prayers and instructions that should, all being well, keep the three of us safe from spiritual harm and prevent any unwanted hangers-on from catching a ride back with us.

As for Lesley, she's already dozing off, with a contented smile on her tired face. Tomorrow the three of us will be leaving Cornwall, and then going our separate ways — until Bodmin Jail calls us back once more for a second encounter.

CHAPTER TWELVE
Round Two

A year comes and goes in what feels to me like little more than the blink of an eye. I spend the remainder of 2018 investigating a number of other haunted locations, this time in my adopted home country, the United States. Malvern Manor in Iowa, said to be haunted by the ghost of a hanged girl; the Villisca Ax Murder House (also in Iowa), an ordinary-looking home in which an entire family was butchered in a night of appalling savagery; and the Farnsworth House at Gettysburg, located right at the heart of one of the world's bloodiest battlefields. These are just a few of the places I'm lucky enough to sink my teeth into when I return from Cornwall.

But Bodmin Jail is always there, lurking at the back of my mind. As dark and foreboding as the place was, I'm surprised to find that it has also exerted a strange attraction on me. Stephen and I both discuss the matter one evening, after I have assisted him in performed a ritual of cleansing at the home of one of our clients (a single mother who, along with her three children, believed that she was being terrorized by an unseen entity). We both feel drawn to the old jail, though neither of us can quite put our finger on the reason why. After talking about it in depth, we agree that there is a sense of unfinished business still lingering where the jail is concerned.

Whatever the reason, we can't wait to get back there, and that's exactly what happens the following year, some thirteen months after we had first set foot in what I firmly believe to be one of the world's most haunted jails. It's now March of 2019, and we're coming back with an even bigger team for two more nights of whatever Bodmin Jail cares to throw at us.

None of us are remotely prepared for what happens this time.

If landing at Heathrow Airport always feels like coming home, then walking through the front door of the Jamaica Inn takes that feeling to the next level. Two-thirds of my team — the entire international component — have elected to stay there this time.

The inn looks, smells, and more importantly *feels* just the same as it always has. I'm instantly comfortable, and after dropping our luggage off at the room, my wife and I are ready to spend some quality time with our friends. We gather in the bar and order some food. Talk soon turns to the reason we're all here: Bodmin Jail.

I'm happy to be working with a team of very experienced paranormal investigators, all of them people I know and trust. They bring a diverse set of backgrounds and skill-sets to the table, and I'm interested to see how things are going to play out with twice as many investigators as were present last year.

Penny is a fellow writer who hosts the *Haunted Histories* podcast, which is how we first met. She's well-known for conducting in-depth research into the background of any haunted location she visits, and also wrote the foreword for this book. Penny's very much at home inside the gym, and likes to lift regularly. This might explain why there are so many pictures on the Internet of her squatting in the doorways of various haunted locations.

She had her own strange experience at Bodmin Jail, which took place when she visited on a hot summer's day several years before. Along with her husband, Penny was on holiday in Cornwall with her two children, who were 4 years old and 9 months old, respectively. While he took the children to the park, Penny decided to spent a little time poking around Bodmin Jail. She'd heard rumors about it being haunted, and coupled with its fascinating history, the jail sounded like just her kind of place.

After buying a ticket and making her way inside, she soon came to a short line of people who were queuing up to look inside one particular cell. While she was waiting to take a look herself, she suddenly heard a woman's voice speaking very clearly and distinctly into her ear. It said the words, *"I couldn't help it. I had no choice."*

This wasn't somebody in the line talking to her. The words were spoken from directly behind her, and had been said in what she recognized as being a Cornish accent. The voice had sounded remorseful and sad. Penny turned around, only to find absolutely nobody standing there. The corridor was completely empty.

Finally reaching the cell in question, she found that it had once belonged to Selena Wadge, who had been executed at Bodmin Jail for murdering her own child — supposedly at the behest of her lover, or so she later claimed.

To make matters even more interesting, it has been said that the spirit of Selena Wadge will make her presence known, most often to children or to mothers, particularly those with very young children themselves. Perhaps she feels some sort of affinity with them, believing that they might have a little sympathy for her plight.

Walking a little further into the building, she was taken by surprise and physically shoved backwards out of another cell. The shove was forceful enough that she had to put her hands out in order to keep her balance. Penny was immediately convinced that whoever — or *whatever* — entity was currently active in that cell, it was an extremely unpleasant being indeed. "This thing hated every single person who was in the jail," she recalls later. The lingering sense of hatred stayed with her long afterward, and after a little careful questioning, I'm able to localize her experience to that part of the upper floor in which Kirsten thought she had seen my body and mannerisms transform into those of somebody else.

She also noticed the smell of burning matches in the oldest part of the jail. Thinking nothing of it at the time, it was only afterward that she would learn that other visitors have reported the very same odor. Penny was told the smell usually meant that the spirits of the former prison guards were about.

Penny needed absolutely no convincing that Bodmin Jail

was haunted. Now she was looking forward to spending some more time there, and seeing whether anybody else might try to communicate with her.

The rest of my team is a diverse and motley bunch of individuals, all of whom have their own contributions to make toward our investigation.

MJ has a wide footprint in the paranormal field. In addition to running Sage Paracon, one of the very best paranormally-themed conventions in the world, MJ also consults on a lot of television shows, such as the UK-based episodes of *Paranormal Lockdown,* to name just one. She is an experienced investigator and a sensitive. When MJ speaks, one can still hear traces of her South African accent. Unlike Penny, this is her first time at Bodmin Jail, but it won't be the last.

Wes works as a corrections officer back home in his native Canada, and has flown out specially to join us at Bodmin Jail. I'm intrigued to see what effect bringing a prison guard into a place like this is going to have on the paranormal activity. I suspect that it will either quieten things down or ramp them up. My money's on the latter. Wes is tall, stocky, and powerfully built. He manages to turn the word "tower" into a verb. Despite his sometimes-imposing demeanor, however, he turns out to be a warm and friendly fellow, extremely polite and respectful.

Stephen is back, and has brought two compatriots with him from across the pond. Sharon and Jill are both experienced investigators, and although they'll also be fighting with the ever-present jet lag, I'm confident that they will be valuable assets over the course of the next few nights. I've worked with them both before and am interested to see how they approach this particular case.

I'm just as delighted to find that Gaynor and Lesley are also back for more. It's good to have more friends and trusted colleagues along. There's also the happy prospect of Lesley taking care of the tea, something she takes always great pride in doing – even if she does pretend that it's an annoyance.

Our first night is Sunday, March 17th. Returning to Bodmin Jail feels like coming back to visit an old friend, albeit one with a dark and possibly malicious side to it. It's six o'clock in the evening when the team walk through the high stone gateway that most of us know so well, and it's almost as if we have never left. Stephen and I exchange a knowing smile. We're both thinking the exact same thing: how fortunate we are to be granted access to this beautiful old place again.

It's wonderful to see Kirsten too. Mark has moved on to pastures new, but we're happy and grateful for the chance to catch up with at least one of our Cornish friends. There are hugs and introductions all round. Then Kirsten leads us back through the tea rooms and into the jail itself.

One of the first things we talk about is what has happened in the past year — more specifically, why haven't I had a visit from the enigmatic spirit lady? She had promised to drop in at my home and make her presence known (something that my wife really wasn't particularly thrilled to find out about) but to the very best of my knowledge, she hadn't shown up. There certainly wasn't a clear sign that would serve as a calling card, which she had promised to leave once she had dropped in. Kirsten has a theory as to why that might be the case, and it's one that leaves a sour taste in my mouth.

"I think it's entirely possible that she isn't a woman at all," she explains gravely. "In fact, I no longer think she's necessarily human."

That stops me dead in my tracks. It's something that I haven't really considered up 'til now. With me being me, however, I can't resist cracking a joke. "I always knew that if I did this for long enough, I'd finally get a succubus." The succubus is said to be a spirit which appears in the form of a beautiful female, and has sex with men (and sometimes women) when they're lying in bed at night.

"He sounds *way* too keen about that." Gaynor rolls her eyes. But all jokes aside, Kirsten gives me a look that tells me I should probably be taking this a little more seriously. She may well be right. Fortunately, the ritual of spiritual protection that Stephen guided us through last time was designed to prevent any negative entities from connecting with us, or attaching themselves to us in any way. This might be the reason why I haven't heard a peep out of the Victorian-era lady over the past 12 months.

"I made a *very* conscious effort to try and connect with her again over the past few months," Kirsten continues, "and we've had a significant number of visitors to the jail tell us that they've seen the apparitions of both a woman and a child here."

"Did anybody ever report seeing them before our encounter with them last year?" I ask. Kirsten shakes her head.

"No, and ever since then, people have been hearing the sound of a woman screaming, crying, and yelling.

Personally, I think that's her...or *it*. Please understand that this isn't a living person who has died and is now in spirit form. This is a negative entity, something born out of negative energy, and it has never been human. That's something entirely different. You're very lucky that it *hasn't* been able to reach you at home. But there's a good reason for that."

"Which is?"

"The negative energies here at the jail are confined here. They are locked into this space."

"Just as the prisoners once were?"

"Exactly." She nods.

This is sounding less and less like good news with every passing sentence. I try to follow her theory to its next logical step, because a new cause for concern has just reared its head.

"Now that I'm back, Kirsten, is she — sorry, is *it* going to be here...waiting?"

"Oh my gosh, yes. Absolutely." She looks me straight in the eye, and all traces of humor are now gone. "You're going to need to be *very* careful this time. It *knew* you were coming back."

"How could it possibly have known that?"

"That's down to me," she admits. "I talk to the building all the time, you see. I said to it, 'Hey, do you remember those guys who came all the way from America? Well, they're coming back here later this week.' It knows that you are coming. *The jail itself* knows that you are coming. And here you are."

I let out a breath I hadn't realized I was holding. Kirsten has just given me a lot to think about, and I don't have time to process that right now. There's a paranormal investigation to be run.

Rubbing my hands together, I declare that it's time for us to get down to work. Once again, we're working out of the break room, and Lesley is still the designated refreshment specialist (it's a catchier title than 'Tea Wallah'). We cache all of our equipment in there, intending to take out only what we need for each session. Kirsten assures us that we're all locked in, so there's no possibility of human intruders disturbing us tonight.

The first order of business is a quick tour for those who haven't been here before. MJ is insistent on not being told any details, in order to avoid prejudicing herself and her sensitive abilities. I respect that approach, and make sure not to tell her anything I know about the jail or its haunting.

Ever the historian, Penny is drawn to every single display case and information plaque like a moth to a flame. She may have been to Bodmin Jail before, but didn't have the time to go into much detail with her studies, and she's clearly very happy to be back.

Wes, for his part, is viewing everything through the lens of a prison officer. For him, this is something akin to a Busman's Holiday. He has an appreciation for old prisons like this, and he seems to be perfectly at home.

Lesley, God love her, is already working on the tea. She really is priceless, and after everybody that wants one has gotten a cup, we all go on a brief tour, covering the layout of the jail from a health and safety point of view. The jail is dimly-lit after dark, and the last thing we want is somebody taking a fall and hurting themselves.

As we congregate outside the break room afterward, a couple of our group catch sight of something moving in the shadows at the far end of the hallway. Whatever it was had emerged from the room on the left, the same place in which we had done the glass work session the year before, and darted quickly across into the opposite doorway. A quick search of both rooms turns up nothing.

It looks like we're off to the races.

CHAPTER THIRTEEN
"It's Not a 'Who.' It's a 'What.'"

With the safety tour now over, we break up into smaller groups and disperse ourselves throughout the building. MJ, Penny, Wes, and I head downstairs to the basement. It's every bit as dark and gloomy as I remember it from last year.

"There's somebody in here that will try and jump you," MJ says as we enter the double-hanging room. "This person wants *in.*"

"Is it a he or a she?" I ask for clarification.

"He." She goes on to explain that if somebody who was gifted in a mediumistic sense were to let their guard down in this room, the aggressive male entity would jump right into them as soon as they were vulnerable.

"It's 1.2 degrees cooler in here than outside." Wes is taking baseline readings with a Mel-Meter. I don't think that a little over a degree in temperature variance would be significant, but it's still good to keep track of these things.

Penny is picking up on the presence of the unseen man too. "My gut feeling is that he's following us. There's something in this room that he wants." There's a pained look on her face, one that hadn't been there when we first came down the stairs a few moments ago. I ask her if she's alright. "I've got a pounding headache. It just came on, the minute we entered this room."

Deciding to put up what she refers to as her 'barriers,' Penny winces and says that she can now feel the man on her back. Both she and MJ agree that this is definitely a strong male energy, and not a very nice one at that. Wes and I hang back and let them do their thing. They're both strong women and refuse to be chased away by anybody, least of all the spirit of a dead man.

"This energy feels like it's trying to overpower me," she adds. MJ nods vigorously.

"Yes, overpowering. Exactly."

After hanging out for a little longer, we go out into the hallway and make for the treadwheel. Then we head on up to the second floor. After we've been up there for a few minutes, I notice that MJ appears to be zoning out. I nudge her.

"Sorry," she says, blinking her eyes back into focus. "There's something sitting on the stairs over there. I'm trying to figure out what it is."

"It?"

"Yes. It's not a who. It's a *what.*"

I turn around to look. The stairs are totally empty, but many people have reported getting nervous in that specific area, experiencing the feeling that they might get pushed down the steps by something unseen.

MJ draws in a deep breath. "It's an elemental."

Penny and I exchange a look of surprise. Even Wes appears taken aback. Elementals are said to be inhuman entities that are usually associated with places of nature — streams, pools, lakes, forests, trees, and suchlike. Stories and folklore surrounding them go back many hundreds of years. What would one be doing on the staircase at Bodmin Jail?

"What's it doing?" I ask.

"Pretending to be a child."

The spirits of children *are* said to haunt the jail, which is not surprising when you think about the fact that more than a few were incarcerated here back in the day. My mind goes back to the spirit woman and her child from last year's glass work session, especially now that Kirsten has raised the suspicion that one or both of them might not have been human. Could this child-like form that MJ is describing be the same boy Kirsten interacted with a year ago — the one that was rather foolishly invited to drop in on me at home?

I don't like that idea. Not one little bit.

"It's trying to draw you in," MJ goes on. "Tugging at your heartstrings, so that it can gain your trust."

Wes is lurking in the shadows off to my right. He's glowering at the staircase, as if silently daring the elemental to show itself.

"It doesn't come up here," says MJ.

"Then I'm going to go down there." I hand Penny my cell phone, and ask her to please take some photographs. My hope is that I might get some sort of photographic evidence if I get closer to where MJ says the thing is.

"Try not to drop my phone."

"Oh, make sure the phone's alright, but don't worry about *me*," Penny snarks, rolling her eyes.

Keeping one hand on the wall to steady myself, I take the stairs one slow step after another. Behind me, I hear the click-click-click of a phone snapping pictures in burst mode. I'm not sensing anything out of the ordinary at the half-way mark.

"Is it aware that we're here?" I ask, looking over my shoulder at MJ. She nods.

"This thing is mischievous, but it's not *evil*," she says. Penny agrees with her, adding that she doesn't get a nasty vibe from the thing. That's a relief to hear, because the stone floor beneath me looks awfully far away, and very, very solid.

"It *has* tripped people up on those stairs," says MJ.

"Then how can you say it's not evil?" I ask, leaning against the wall a little more heavily. "You could *kill* somebody by doing that."

"But that's not how it thinks. The elemental is playing. It's a prankster, not a monster."

I'm getting nothing tangible, so Penny offers to swap out with me. She takes my place on the staircase, and now it's my turn to take the photos. Between us, we manage to blaze off more than fifty shots. None of them show anything anomalous. There are a few minor temperature and EMF fluctuations, according to our instruments, but nothing to write home about, so after ten more minutes have passed, we head back downstairs.

I have a little experiment in mind. The experience that MJ and Penny had with the predatory male energy down in the basement has gotten me thinking. What would happen if I placed another female investigator down there, all on her own, in that exact same location?

In other words, I'd be using her as bait.

Gaynor is always up for a challenge. Without telling her

exactly why, I escort her downstairs to that particular room and ask her to spend fifteen minutes or so alone in there, and then let us know if anything unusual happens. If this sounds a little callous on my part, it's important to remember that Gaynor was a sergeant in the Territorial Army and is more than capable of keeping a cool head in a crisis. In fact, I pity the man — living or dead — that ends up on her bad side. Still, just to be safe, she has her cell phone with her, and the cavalry is just one quick text, phone call, or yell away.

She pulls up the only available chair, sits down, and starts a voice recorder running, cheerily waving me off as I go back up to the break room. Gaynor spends some time trying to establish a rapport with any spirits that might be present, speaking to them in her usual outgoing and friendly manner.

"My phone battery is at 75%," she offers. "Would you like to take some of that energy and use it to say hello to me?"

Sadly, there are no takers. Gaynor experiences nothing like the kind of oppression that Penny and MJ reported. It's a peaceful and quiet quarter of an hour. At the end of it, MJ, Lesley, and Wes go down to join her, adding a little extra energy into the mix. They set up a few REM-PODS at strategic intervals around the basement. This device generates an energy field which, some people believe, can be manipulated by certain entities, causing it to flash and emit an annoyingly high-pitched warble.

"We invite anybody that's down here to come forward and talk to us," Wes booms. "Were you an inmate? A guard? A corrections officer—"

"*Prison* officer," Gaynor corrects him.

"Thank you. Got to remember the lingo over here." Wes is reminded that although he is in a prison, he isn't in his native Canada tonight. "Some people must have some stories here. What's yours? My name is Wes. I'm a jailor, from Canada." He goes on to introduce his companions, one by one, then respectfully encourages any unseen residents of the jail to step close to one of the REM-PODS.

"There's a man standing in the doorway," says MJ. "I just saw him peeking around the corner. Why don't you come and join our conversation? We just want to know who you are."

"He's standing by my shoulder, isn't he?" Gaynor asks. MJ nods in affirmation. "I can feel him." Suddenly, she gasps. "He's *right* on me. Okay...look, I'm happy to give you some of my energy, but please leave some for me."

The entity obligingly backs away into the open doorway.

MJ suggests a burst EVP session, which everybody agrees to. Sadly, nothing turns up on the playback. Perhaps whoever's down there with them doesn't feel like talking, preferring to hang back in the shadows and watch. Next up is a Spirit Box session. The tinny hiss of a radio sweeping from channel to channel floods the basement. Gaynor tries to coax the man she still believes is standing in the doorway into talking to her.

Apparently, nobody wants to communicate through the box either, yet MJ and Gaynor are both insistent that they are not all alone down there. Wes and Lesley have their eyes on the hallway outside, but they aren't seeing anything moving out there.

There's an audible exhalation that MJ insists doesn't come from any of the team. Wes is the only one that hears it, however, and he marks it on the audio log for later review. The sigh is indeed picked up, but it's impossible to prove that it didn't originate from one of the four sets of human lungs in the area, so Ockham's Razor (which states that, given two competing explanations, the simplest one is most likely to be correct) means that we have to throw it out as possible evidence.

"I think it's possible that because you're a jailor, they're keeping you at arm's length," MJ posits to Wes.

"Then let me excuse myself for a minute." He ducks out into the hallway and puts some space between himself and the ladies, but stays within earshot just in case he's needed.

MJ thinks she hears a female voice whispering, but it isn't captured on any of the voice recorders that have been continuously running since the start of the session.

"Holy shit!" MJ suddenly yells. "*F*** right off!*"

Wes is right there in a flash. Gaynor and Lesley come over to make sure she's okay. MJ apologizes for her sudden outburst, and explains that something just ran its fingers through her hair. Wes asks if she wants to step out for a moment, but MJ vehemently refuses. She's not about to let herself be intimidated. She isn't that kind of person.

Everybody begins to feel cold all of a sudden. According to the Mel-Meter, the temperature has dropped by four degrees.

"Whoever just grabbed MJ's hair, why don't you try and touch somebody else's?" Lesley issues an open challenge. Nobody else is singled out for special treatment, however. For some reason, MJ appears to have become the focus of this male entity's attention.

It's odd that when Gaynor was all alone, at her most vulnerable, she felt absolutely nothing out of the ordinary. When Lesley, Wes, and MJ arrived, she instantly became aware of the presence in the room along with them.

The group comes back upstairs to share their experience with the rest of the team. Along the way, Wes and MJ are chatting. MJ is running a voice recorder continually, as most of us are, and now it pays dividends. On playback, Wes can be heard talking about his habit of moving quietly, almost stealthily while on an investigation ("I don't mean to sneak up on people") when a dusky, sibilant female voice is suddenly heard to interject *"Hey!"* The tone of voice is enthusiastic, and fits Wes's comment perfectly; almost as if an unseen person *has* snuck up on Wes and MJ, saw a brief opportunity to speak up, and mock-whispered *"Hey!"* to announce their presence. It's an intriguing EVP. The question now becomes: will there be any more?

Lesley, MJ, Wes and Gaynor head upstairs. It's a decision that Lesley will quickly come to regret. A few minutes later, she arrives back in the break room, looking distinctly troubled and paler than usual. I ask her what's wrong. She seems ever so slightly confused, but after taking a moment to compose herself, she tells us what she can remember.

She had been sitting on the staircase between the second and third floors. They thought that they heard the sound of a child's voice coming from somewhere in the darkness, and set about trying to track down the source.

At this point, Lesley appears to have suffered some kind of blackout. There is a missing section of her memory, no longer than a minute or so, but still a period of amnesia nonetheless. The next thing she remembers is a very concerned Gaynor leaning over her, making sure that she was alright.

I have personally seen this happen to Lesley once before, at an allegedly haunted house in Hull: 39 De Grey Street, also known as 'the Hostel.' We were sitting in a room full of mirrors, inviting any spirits that were present to communicate with us, when suddenly Lesley's face went slack. To coin a phrase, the lights were on but nobody was home. After twenty seconds of Lesley not responding to my voice, I gently nudged her back to awareness once more. In that case, too, she had no recollection of the brief period of amnesia.

Lesley sits down and has a reassuring chat with Sharon. In no time at all, she is back to her old self again, chirpy and happy-go-lucky. Stephen works with her on a little spiritual protection, helping to bolster her defenses just in case something from the jail was attempting to influence her in some way.

Wes, Gaynor and MJ have been conducting their own Estes Method EVP session at the top of the staircase near the second-floor landing. They both look surprised when I emerge from the floor below. MJ explains that the Spirit Box they had been using had just said the words *"He's coming up,"* no more than a few seconds before I arrived. I had indeed come up. This sounded like an intelligent notification to them that I was climbing the stairs.

It's only days later, when I review my notes from the prior year's investigation, that I remember Kirsten telling us that she had been taken over by the spirit of a Cornishman up on the second floor, a spirit that had spoken through her mouth and given everybody a distinct warning: something was coming up the staircase from down below.

I take the opportunity to ask my team-mates about the incident with Lesley a few minutes prior. A few new and disturbing details come to light. Gaynor tells me that as Lesley was undergoing her period of apparent blackout, her face appeared to physically change, becoming fatter as though it was swelling up. I can't help but wonder if this was simply a trick of the light, which seems the most reasonable explanation, though it's impossible to say for sure. The phenomenon of facial (and full-body) transfiguration has been reported many times at Bodmin Jail.

Gaynor went over to Lesley in order to make sure that she was okay, and once Lesley snapped out of whatever state she was in, she became upset and began to cry — again, something very out of character for her. During the drive to the jail that night, Gaynor reveals, Lesley had been on her usual fine form, singing raucously along to an ABBA song on the radio. Her typical happy-go-lucky affect had changed just as soon as she set foot inside the jail. That observation strikes me as being both interesting and concerning in equal measure, and I resolve to keep a closer eye on her as the night goes on.

Now it's my turn for an unanticipated personal experience. It's a few minutes before midnight, and I feel the call of nature. Making my way downstairs to the ground floor men's room, I step into one of the stalls, lock the door, and, well...you know. As I'm sitting there, thinking about nothing in particular, I hear the door open. It has to be either Wes or Stephen coming in. I cough loudly, the universal signal for "Hey, I'm in here, this stall is occupied." There's no response. Nor, I realize, are there any footsteps coming into the men's room. Just silence.

Finishing up as quickly as I can, I poke my head out from around the door. The men's room is completely deserted. I test the door. It's fairly heavy. There's no way a freak gust of wind would have been able to blow it open. Not that there is much in the way of air movement in this part of the jail anyway.

Reaching into my hip pocket, I pull out a voice recorder and start it running. Pretty much everything I do at the jail is being recorded for posterity, but I draw the line when it comes to the call of nature. I do a very quick burst session, but nobody speaks up in the form of an EVP.

I head back to the break room. Stephen is elsewhere in the building, but Wes is there. He vehemently denies having been anywhere near the men's room in the past hour.

MJ recounts her own bathroom experience, which took place a short while before mine. She had gone into the ladies' room and found the faucet in the sink blasting hot water into the bowl at maximum flow. None of the women present in the jail tonight were responsible for it, and I find it interesting that the two restrooms adjoin one another, being separated only by a single wall. There's no way it's a coincidence that both a male and a female investigator experience something weird in their respective toilets, all within a very short period of time.

I'm tempted to make a Moaning Myrtle joke, but this isn't Hogwarts and it's time to move on to the next part of our investigation. I fancy the idea of spending some quality time on my own down in the basement. Perhaps the aggressive male spirit that was so fond of MJ will come and say hello to me. I go down to the same room and settle into the chair that still sits in the center, stuffing my hands into the pockets of my jacket in order to keep them warm. It's starting to get extremely cold, and I'm glad that I've bundled up in several layers.

Heavy footsteps thump across the ceiling above me. Once again, I'm reminded of just how far sound carries inside the jail. You'd think that all that stone would dampen any extraneous noise down, but it doesn't. Sometimes, it feels like being in an echo chamber, listening to the sound of voices and movement from the floor above.

I try to make casual conversation, inviting him or anybody else to come forward and get acquainted. There's no sound at all save for the occasional dripping of water coming from the hallway outside. I stifle a yawn and mark it for the audio recorder, so that it's not mistaken for an EVP later on.

It's as dark as dark can be down here, and I expect to feel some sort of fear, or at the very least a sense of nervousness. After all, I'm in the basement of one of the world's most haunted prisons, all on my own with the lights out. I ought to feel vulnerable, at the very least, but the truth is that the atmosphere feels peaceful to me, almost flat. If I have any company here in the room, it's doing a very good job of keeping itself hidden.

I sit quietly for half an hour, letting my brain slip into a neutral state that's somewhere between daydreaming and meditation. Nothing happens. Finally, groaning in that way that all middle-aged men do when they stand up, I make my way back upstairs to the break room again. I must look cold because Lesley makes a cup of tea to warm me up a bit without me even asking for it.

I don't consider the time I spent in the basement to be wasted. We've learned a valuable piece of information: whatever it is that's down there doesn't seem to target people who are on their own. Neither Gaynor or I were the recipients of anything approaching the creepy hair stroke that MJ was subjected to.

The session now over, I spend some time hanging out with MJ in the break room, watching the monitors. At the end of the hallway on the left, a glass work session is going on. Lesley, Gaynor, Penny, and Kirsten are all working together in a group. MJ tells me that she is disturbed by the energies that are being stirred up in that room.

"I just don't like it," she says. "My Spidey Sense is tingling."

As things turn out, she has good reason to be concerned.

One of the participants is convinced that her dead sister came through during the glass session. In fact, she is so sure of it that she has been moved to tears. It's a very sensitive situation, and what worries me about it is that with glass work — just like the spirit board, or any other purported tool for spirit communication — it's almost impossible to verify the true identity of the communicator. It's a bit like a fake Facebook profile: you only have the other person's word for who they really are, and some people delight in misrepresenting themselves.

Is it possible that the deceased sister of one of my colleagues really followed her to Bodmin Jail tonight and used an empty glass to speak with her? Yes, I do believe that such a thing *might* be possible. But I also have to caution everybody that they could also have been dealing with an entity that was lying to them, in order to achieve its own ends— whatever they might have been.

On the other hand, one participant tells us that a question was answered during the session which only she herself could have known — well, either she or another dead relative of hers. It's interesting, most definitely, but one possible theory for the way in which these things work is that the subconsciousness of the participants is behind it all, with those people whose fingers are on the glass itself unwittingly guiding it to tell the correct answer.

I don't want to be cruel, and rob my friend of an idea that she has already begun to cherish: that they have been visited by a lost loved one here at Bodmin Jail tonight. But I also encourage them to take any information received with a huge grain of salt, a policy that is always wise when applied to the field of paranormal field research.

It's not that I don't sympathize; in fact, very much to the contrary. Having lost several loved ones myself, I'd give almost anything to speak with them again. That introduces a huge amount of bias, and is therefore something we have to guard ourselves against.

"I always recommend that when things get personal during an investigation, you step away from it," I tell her gently. "It's a very moving experience, but this could also be dangerous for you."

When it comes to something so intimate in nature, I know that it's not my place to rain on their parade. Having given my unsolicited advice, I decide to leave things where they stand, and let that particular sleeping dog lie.

We gather together and go over our experiences from the night so far. In addition to everything else that has happened already, MJ has picked up an interesting tapping sound on her voice recorder, one that she can't easily explain away. She didn't hear it at the time, only noticing it during playback. It also emerges that a while ago, when Lesley and MJ were standing outside having a smoke, they heard a loud, guttural growl coming from thin air right next to Lesley.

"You're sure it wasn't Lesley?" I ask MJ. "She can get a bit fierce when she's provoked."

Lesley waves at me, but doesn't use all of her fingers.

"It definitely wasn't her," MJ insists. "It was loud and sounded human-*ish*, not like an animal."

That's good to hear. Back in the States, we worry about things such as mountain lions on our investigations, but jolly old England doesn't have anything along those lines, and certainly not inside the walls of a prison that's totally sealed off from the outside world.

"Directly above where you were standing is the window of a cell that once terrified one of our visitors," Kirsten tells Lesley. She recounts the experience of a man who insisted that there was nothing paranormal going on at Bodmin Jail, but who also maintained that he kept hearing something scratching away at the walls inside that particular cell, "like a big rat or something." Leaning his head and shoulders into the doorway for a closer look, the man suddenly yelped as though stung and practically flew out of the cell. After she calmed him down, he told Kirsten that he could feel a presence leaning in closely to his face, as if an invisible something was staring him down. The straw that broke the camel's back was a low growl, which Kirsten imitates for us to great effect.

"That's it!" Lesley and MJ exclaim at the same time.

Things start to wind down after this. It's our first night, and we're already impressed with the jail, but our own energy levels are starting to flag. You can only run on caffeine and excitement for so long. Finally, we agree to call it a night — or rather, a morning, because the birds are starting to sing outside when we step out into the cool pre-dawn air.

Everybody gets together for a survivors' photo, our now-traditional way of marking the end of a night's investigation. Stephen, Jill, and Sharon had left early, too worn out to continue. The rest of us squeeze into the frame for a selfie, with the brooding edifice of the jail looming high above us.

After she lets us all out of the front gate, Kirsten announces that she has the feeling tomorrow night will be the big night. It's going to be our final night at Bodmin Jail, and the energies are building up to something.

As things turn out, she's absolutely right. But I have no idea that the old prison is going to catch me completely off-guard, in a rather unpleasant way.

CHAPTER FOURTEEN
Aggressive

The team sleeps the rest of the day away, and reconvenes for dinner (which is technically breakfast) later that afternoon. Although we don't have any factual basis for it, there's a general consensus that tonight is going to be *the night*. There's a common feeling that the jail has been building its energy, and we're all eager to see whether Kirsten's prediction of the night before will be proven correct.

Bodmin Jail is beginning to feel like a home away from home for me now. As I park the rental car on the hill leading up to it, I realize there are butterflies in my stomach, that sense of anticipation which is difficult to explain to those who don't do the strange things that we paranormal investigators do. Wes and I carry our equipment into the jail, where we're once again greeted by Kirsten.

"Where would you like to begin?" she asks, once all of the equipment has been set out, loaded with fresh batteries, and declared ready for use. The entire team is in agreement. Everybody wants to begin in the one place we didn't cover last night: the hanging pit

We're then given a serious health and safety brief,

emphasizing just how treacherous the climb down into the hanging pit can be. Then we head out there to experience it for ourselves. Stephen, Sharon, and Jill haven't arrived yet, but the rest of us are chomping at the bit to get on.

"The rope isn't the original, of course," Kirsten explains as she unlocks the gate, pointing toward the noose dangling over the trapdoor, "but the lever is. This was used to send Valeri Giovanni and William Hampton to their deaths a hundred years ago, so please treat it with respect."

Nobody needs to be told twice.

Satisfied that everybody is taking it seriously, she allows us to make the descent down into the pit, which has been left uncovered. With a mini-flashlight in my mouth to light my way, I start climbing down. It's every bit as dank and chilly as I remember it, but at least the ground is slightly drier than last year. The mud and water are only toe-deep this time. Bodmin hasn't been subject to the same hellacious rain storms this year.

It's a little crowded once everybody reaches the bottom — I'd say 'cosy,' but that's a difficult word to apply to a place of execution — and we all push ourselves back against the walls.

With all flashlights now extinguished, all we have is the

ambient light from the night sky to see by. We run a quick burst EVP session, but nothing unusual turns up on the replay. The team takes photographs from all angles, catching plenty of dust and floating particulate matter, but nothing of any real interest shows up.

Despite the fact that there isn't a cloud in the sky, the water level is starting to rise around our feet. Once everybody has had their fill of the pit, we clamber back out again. When I'm back at ground level again, I catch Kirsten giving me a very odd look. I'm about to ask her what's wrong, when Gaynor, Penny, and MJ ask me to take some pictures of them. By the time we've finished snapping photos, the strange expression on her face has completely slipped my mind. I won't find out the reason for it until the end of the night.

Something uninvited came up with us.

One investigative technique I'm particularly fond of is that of the *era cue*. This is a process of using something that would emotionally resonate with people from a particular era in time, and hopefully will stimulate them to interact with the researcher. To this end, Kirsten has the bright idea of staging a mock execution.

Showing her typical sense of pluck, Gaynor gamely volunteers to play the part of the condemned criminal. Wes and I are obvious choices to stand in for the warders; we're both big, burly guys, and escorting convicts is his everyday bread and butter.

Beginning at the top of the jail steps, we take Gaynor by the arm and frog-march her down the path toward the execution shed. Kirsten is running the show, calling out instructions as we go. I'm suddenly acutely aware that we are literally walking in the footsteps of two dead men.

We escort Gaynor up to the platform, helping her keep her balance along the way.

"Executioner ready?" Kirsten asks, looking over at Wes.

"READY!" the big Canadian booms in a voice so loud that I nearly jump out of my skin. It echoes from the walls of the execution shed. We're going for realism, and Wes is obliging by flipping the switch that sends him straight into prison officer mode. There's an intensity to him now that wasn't there before.

We place a makeshift hood over Gaynor's head. Now she's standing there at the edge of the hanging pit, swaying slightly because she's devoid of sight, and her sense of balance has been impaired. We stop short of actually placing the noose around her neck. That would be a bridge too far, and would cross the line from evoking memories of executions long past into plain disrespect, something that none of us is willing to do.

Gaynor really is showing her grit. I can only imagine what she must feel like, rendered totally blind, held tightly on either arm in a vice-like grip, in a genuine place of execution. Psychologically speaking, it has to be quite unpleasant.

My train of thought is broken by the mournful tolling of a bell. It's Kirsten. She tells us that after a hanging had taken place, the Bodmin Jail bell, which is said to be some two hundred years old, was rung once to announce to the public that the death sentence had been carried out successfully. The ringing of phantom bells has been heard by a number of visitors over the years, and I wonder whether it's an after-echo of this particular bell.

We let Gaynor stand there for a few minutes, soaking up the intense atmosphere. If she's afraid, she isn't showing a hint of it. Finally, we uncover her head and help her down. It's dark enough that her eyes don't take long to adjust.

Penny is taking photographs, recording events for posterity. When she's finished, she puts the camera away and we stand around, discussing the history of executions here at Bodmin.

"Did somebody just take a photo?" Penny suddenly asks. Everybody shakes their head. Nobody has a camera or a phone out. "But there was a flash — right over here. I *saw* it."

Penny insists that she witnessed a sudden flare of bright light, just for a split-second, a few feet away from us. It was as if somebody took a photograph using a flash. I'm tempted to write it off as being something as mundane as car headlights, but thanks to the high walls of the jail, headlight beams don't tend to penetrate into the courtyard. Something else to chalk up to the high strangeness of Bodmin Jail.

I'm beginning to feel a little somber and downcast. That's not difficult to explain. The hanging pit is a very maudlin place, as befits its sole purpose. Perhaps the atmosphere of the place has managed to seep into me somehow. I try to brush it off and go about my business.

Stephen and his cohorts arrive. Taking me aside, he tells me that when we arrived at the jail the night before, he could smell sulfur as soon as he stepped foot inside. Having worked with him for many years, I know that he believes this to signify the presence of some type of dark entity. My mind instantly jumps to the supposed female my team and I had communicated with the year before, an entity which Kirsten now believes to be something entirely different. The good news is that he can't smell anything amiss tonight, so perhaps whatever it was has lost interest in us and is going to leave us well alone.

"We've experienced a smell like that for the past three months or so," Kirsten declares. "One night, the whole building reeked so much that we all had to take a break from the investigation. Every part of the jail just *stank.*"

Before I can diplomatically raise the possibility of the odor perhaps coming from a backed-up drain or something similar, Kirsten beats me to the punch, pointing out that if there was a natural explanation for it, the smell should be much more persistent, and would turn up more regularly than it actually does. The sulfurous stink doesn't seem to bother anybody during the daylight hours, when staff are going about the business of keeping the jail open for the public. Once night falls, and paranormal investigations kick off, the smell comes back.

For now, though, the jail smells perfectly normal.

"That was quite the night," she continues. "People were

getting very, very grumpy with one another. Some got extremely agitated, snapping at each other without any kind of reason...it was just *horrible."*

That's food for thought. Could something in the jail — perhaps even the jail itself — have been influencing them?

Because some of our colleagues want to conduct a Spirit Box session on one of the upper levels, Stephen, Kirsten, and I head down to the level below the ground floor in order to minimize noise contamination. We wander from room to room. From the look on his face, Stephen is in 'psychic bloodhound' mode, following his instincts and trying to dial in on some of the energies present in the jail.

"There's something here." He stops dead in his tracks. "Mostly residual energy, I think."

"Positive or negative?" I want to know.

"Both. But the more recent stuff has been darker. Especially two or three weeks ago"

Kirsten is impressed. "That's absolutely spot on."

"Let's hear the story."

There is, she tells us, an entity that some refer to as 'the old tramp.' For American readers, the term 'tramp' refers to a homeless person in this particular context. His presence is often associated with an odor that smells like excrement or urine.

"It was absolutely *disgusting,*" Kirsten wrinkles her nose. "So bad, it could almost bring tears to your eyes."

"There's also something down in the basement," he says, changing tack. "Horribly dark, and very, *very* strong."

Kirsten and I exchange a look. The room he describes is the same one in which MJ had her hair pulled the night before. We had deliberately withheld the information from Stephen so that we didn't prejudice his findings.

"I tried to go in there last night," he adds, "but it felt as if there was a door, trying to stop me from going in. An almost tangible barrier. I pushed through it and went into the room, but I immediately became nauseous and had to leave."

"You should go in there with me, Stephen," Kirsten smiles. He chuckles.

"No time like the present," I suggest. The three of us make our way down to the basement, taking it slow and steady in the near-darkness.

"He's coming off as a mean and nasty entity," the priest says as we enter the room.

"*He?* So, it's a human spirit, rather than something non-human?"

"It's a deceased human," he confirms. "And his teeth are

horrible."

"That's because he's British." Being British myself, I feel as if I can get away with a crack like that. My teeth are far from being the perfect pearly whites that many of my American friends have. "Can you describe him?"

"Old. No hair...at least, what hair he has is very thin. His clothes are very unkempt. He doesn't have any shoes. He stays pretty much in this area, and doesn't travel very far. He's keeping his distance from us now."

"Is there any chance he'll talk to us?" I ask, holding up the digital voice recorders. Stephen shakes his head, indicating that he won't. After reviewing the audio later, he is proven to be right.

Wes joins us, and we spend a good forty-five minutes in this room, trying to entice the old man — or any other potential communicator — to come out and talk with us. No joy. But something odd *does* occur for Kirsten and Wes.

"You're morphing," the prison officer says, looking right at Kirsten.

"Into what?"

"Into *him*."

Wes believes that he is seeing her face change, going from a woman in her forties to that of somebody quite a few years older. As mentioned earlier, this phenomenon, that of a person's face seeming to change into that of a completely different person, has been anecdotally documented in quite a few cases. I've even experienced it myself right here at Bodmin Jail. On at least two occasions, I could have sworn that Kirsten's face has become that of a very old woman, the sort of hag-like appearance used to portray witches in fairy tales. The question is, is this a genuine phenomenon or simply the eyes misperceiving an ordinary face in low-light conditions?

Stephen adds that he's also seeing Kirsten start to morph. I'm scrutinizing her carefully, and it looks to me as if she's also growing in stature, thickening about the middle. I blink rapidly, but the effect still seems very real. Trusting a camera more than I do my eyes, I take a photograph. There she is, looking perfectly normal on the screen. Are we all simply feeding into one another's suggestions here, or is something at work that defies conventional understanding?

"He's a good guy," Stephen says, keeping his eyes on Kirsten but speaking about the old man. "He just needs to quit being so darn defensive."

"He can be a bastard," Kirsten chimes in, "but only because he thinks he needs to be."

"He should probably go to confession," adds Stephen.

"Oh, you know what he's saying now? F*** you!" Kirsten fires back. The priest is not taken aback in the slightest.

"Just knock it *off*. Seriously, you're a good guy. Have you ever heard the saying that you can catch more bees with honey than you can with vinegar?"

It's quite a surreal experience. Stephen and Kirsten seem to be able to see and hear this invisible old man. Wes says that he can sense something too, but I have absolutely no extra senses above and beyond the basic five that I was born with. I just hang back and watch the interplay between three people, one of whom is apparently both a) dead and b) somebody I can't see. It's one of the frustrating things about working with sensitives: you're totally reliant upon what they tell you is going on. Sometimes that can be verified objectively, in the form of an EVP or some other hard-to-explain piece of phenomena, but not always.

We're now told that the old man is now pointedly ignoring Stephen, and has instead turned his attention to Wes. "He's showing me how he can take you down," Kirsten tells him. "He thinks he's found your Achilles Heel. Now he's laughing at you."

Even in the darkness, I can see Wes stand a little bit straighter, as though he is getting ready to square off against some kind of threat. "Bring it on," he rumbles.

"What's the Achilles Heel he's referring to?" I ask.

"The mid-calf on his left leg."

"Is that right, Wes?"

"The mid-calf on my *right* leg, actually," Wes corrects her, before daring the old man to do his worst.

"Now there's a woman here," Stephen cuts in. "She's in her, oh, mid-thirties. I think she might be his sister."

"I know her. This is the woman that can calm him," says Kirsten. "He was here as a prisoner during his lifetime, because he was sentenced to jail for beating other men."

"Almost to the point of death," adds Stephen. "*She's* actually the one in charge, not him. She could also rile him up." Suddenly, he stops and sniffs the air. "Do you smell urine?"

Nobody but him can. Stephen insists that he can smell dirt and pee right here in the room with us.

"So, back to this woman..." I steer the conversation back to the mysterious female.

"She's an instigator," Kirsten tells us. "She can set him off when she feels like it, and she's the only one that can control him once he goes off. He's the one that carried the can for it, though, for beating people up in a rage."

"That would make her almost worse than him," I point out.

"Yes, it would," she agrees. "What a bitch. I actually think their relationship might have been incestuous."

"*Ew.*" I make a face. "Suddenly, things have gotten very *Game of Thrones.*"

Kirsten and Stephen agree that the woman has been hanging back on the periphery and just watching us, scoping us out and looking for any sign of weakness.

I check my watch. It's about time for us to see how the others are doing. We carefully retrace our steps toward the staircase. Wes suddenly smells feces on the way out, perhaps a parting shot from our two newly-acquired 'friends.'

Things have gotten interesting during our absence. Penny was standing in the transfer corridor, opposite the tea rooms, running a voice recorder. She heard a series of extremely loud and repeated knocks coming from behind the locked door to the tea rooms. There's no way it could have been a living person. The only human being with a key is Kirsten, and she has been with us the entire time.

"It was so loud, it sounded like somebody running around in there," Penny tells us, hitting the play button on her recorder. Sure enough, the sounds can be easily heard and go on for quite some time. The tea rooms are completely empty, and we don't come up with a good explanation for the sounds.

Now MJ and I both smell an odor that seems very much like sulfur or some similar type of gas to us, in the hallway outside the break room. After hanging around for a minute or two, it suddenly dissipates.

Curiouser and curiouser.

"I have a question for you," MJ suddenly says to Stephen. "Why am I picking up on a heart attack from you?"

I frown, wondering where she's going with this. I know Stephen well enough to be sure that he has never had a heart attack before. His answer to her question drops my jaw.

"Because a friend of mine had a heart attack this morning," he says matter-of-factly.

He takes the question in his stride — perhaps because he's a sensitive conversing with another sensitive? — but I'm quite taken aback. I'm very familiar with the technique of cold reading, in which fraudulent so-called 'psychics' ask a series of open-ended questions until they home in on a key piece of information about their target. But a heart attack is a very specific thing. If MJ were faking this, she could just as easily have asked about a stroke, a head injury, or any one of a hundred other serious medical conditions. This wasn't something that Stephen had shared openly. Hell, even *I* didn't know about it. It wasn't like he'd posted about it on Facebook or made it the subject of discussion at dinner. All things being equal, I'm finding MJ's hit to be quite impressive.

"Oh, I'm so sorry!" she says, placing a hand gently on Stephen's arm.

"It's fine," he demurs. "My friend is going to be okay."

That's good to hear, at least. Now I'm looking at MJ in a whole new light.

Lesley brings me a much-welcome cup of tea. "I don't know how to tell you this," she begins awkwardly, "but all night long, your face has been looking like Play-Doh."

Lovely. I'm being told that my face looks like a compound used for kids to make shapes out of. She explains that my features are blurring and becoming amorphous. We've already encountered something similar to happening earlier on in the night, with Kirsten's face appearing to shift and change form when we were downstairs. Are we all going mad, or is something genuinely weird at work tonight at Bodmin Jail?

Whichever might be the case, Lesley is the next person to be affected. While she's standing outside taking a break, she tells us that she sees a clearly-defined black mass zip past the end of the hallway at high speed. The anomaly doesn't have arms, legs, a head, or any human or animal characteristics at all. Although she's convinced of what she saw, I'm beginning to wonder if the jail isn't starting to play games with our minds.

Sharon and Jill have also experienced something strange. They were working on the same floor as the break room (ground minus one) carrying out a series of burst EVP sessions. Things got interesting in the room at the far end of the hall on the left, the same room used for glass work. From the very first moment they walked into the room, they could feel a sense of pressure inside it, beginning right at the doorway. They decided to employ some dowsing rods in an attempt to better understand what it was that they were dealing with.

"This was not human," Sharon explains to us. "And it

most definitely does *not* like the fact that we recognized it as such. This thing is nasty, and it doesn't like us being aware of its presence."

"It was stand-offish," Jill adds. Sharon agrees.

"So, we forced it to answer us. It did not like that at all."

Something dawns on me that I really don't like. Nevertheless, I have to ask the question. "Is this the kind of thing that would be capable of imitating something or someone else?"

They both nod in unison. I take the next logical step, remembering what had happened to Penny, Gaynor, and Lesley during the glass work session.

"Could it perhaps be guilty of impersonating somebody's deceased loved one?"

"Absolutely," Sharon agrees. "This is on the darker side."

That puts the past events from the glass work room in an entirely different light. I'd been suspicious of what was happening even then, but now I *really* don't like the possibility of something non-human playing mind games with my friends.

Jill takes up the story next. "So, we left the room and came back here toward the break room. That's when I got punched in the back."

My eyebrows shoot up. "Physically? You were physically *punched* in your back?"

Jill's adamant that she was. "The pain was so bad I almost threw up."

After the punch, a painful pressure had flared up across Jill's lower back and kidneys. Caught totally off-guard by the attack, she had begun crying, the pain was so great. Sharon and Stephen helped her through it, and now Jill was almost back to feeling her old self. The influence had obviously shaken her up, but she's not the sort of person to let something like that chase her away.

"Well, tonight was supposed to be the big night, from what we were told," I point out.

"It feels to me like this place is a bubbling cauldron," says MJ. "Right now, things are *just* on the edge...it's been almost too calm in here, and now, shit's about to hit the fan."

MJ goes on to admit that over the past half hour, she has started to feel unusually aggressive. Kirsten had brought in an old book, an item that was reputed to have some negative energies associated with it, and MJ traces her inexplicable anger to the moment when the book first made its appearance. Before then, it was locked in her office at the top of the tower.

I'd been watching her at the time, and had noticed her affect change as soon as Kirsten brought the book into the room. It was the same sort of response a dog gives when its hackles go up, and I'm not sure that she was even consciously aware of it at the time.

"It's on a minor level," Sharon says, "but it's definitely demonic in nature."

I'm careful not to say anything in reply. I respect the right of everybody in the field of paranormal research to hold their own opinions and belief systems. — after all, we are all subject to our own biases, in one form or another, no matter how objective we try to be. I've never been a big fan of the term 'demonic.' To be honest, I think that certain TV shows have gone to that particular well so many times, the word has been grossly over-used. I am open to the possibility that non-human entities may exist, because I think it would be arrogant to assume that all of the so-called spirits that people encounter necessarily belong to dead human beings.

With that being said, it's been my experience that some of the so-called demonic cases out there may have been nothing more than a human spirit lashing out in anger. Objects hurled from shelves, disembodied screams, people getting scratched — all could potentially be signs of an aggressive deceased human being.

To be clear, I'm not saying that demonic entities don't exist. I'm saying that *if* they do, then they are almost certainly less common than some people like to think they are. That's just my two cents, so please take it for what it's worth. It's entirely possible that I'm wrong about this.

One piece of supporting evidence for Sharon's contention is the rank sulfurous smell that is so often reported from inside the jail. Several members of our own group have experienced it for themselves. Some of those who claim to be demonologists state that such smells are associated with the presence of demonic entities. On a slightly more prosaic level, paranormal investigators have reported such smells occurring during outbreaks of poltergeist activity.

"I feel really aggressive," repeats MJ. "I mean, *really* aggressive." Although nobody realizes it at the time, this is a sign of things to come.

CHAPTER FIFTEEN
"You'll Be Back."

For the next rotation, MJ and I head down to the basement together, just the two of us. She immediately picks up on the spirit of the woman that Kirsten and Stephen talked about earlier, the female who they believe controls the more aggressive male entity. Once again, she's sensing some aggression, but this time it's external, rather than something she's feeling personally.

We set up a Spirit Box and set it to a fast sweep rate, hoping to get either the brother or the sister to speak to us. No voices come through the speaker at all, just the random hiss of white noise.

"He's running up to me and stopping right in front of my nose," MJ says. I peer into the blackness, seeing and feeling nothing.

Suddenly there's a chirp. I look down. The recorder I'm holding in my hand has just switched itself off. I had put fresh batteries in it three hours before. They're usually good for at least 24 hours of continuous operation. Now the thing is as dead as a doornail.

I switch it on again and the battery indicator shows a full

charge. This means that we're not talking about a hard-to-explain battery drain — somehow the recorder was manually switched off. I am one hundred percent sure that I didn't switch it off myself. The on/off switch is a slider which has to be slid and held in order for the recorder to be powered off. There's no way it can be done inadvertently.

MJ switches the Spirit Box off so that we can hear our ambient environment a little better. The device isn't doing anything other than irritate us.

"He really doesn't like you, this man," says MJ, looking at somebody that I can't see.

Nnnnn.

It's a grunt, male by the sound of it, and it didn't come from me — it came from thin air, originating from somewhere behind me in the shadows.

We run a quick burst EVP session in an attempt to get this phantom grunter to speak to us, but it's a bust. Things are quietening down in the basement. After a quick discussion, MJ and I agree to change things up a bit and check out one of the upper floors. We collect Lesley along the way and make our way up the spiral staircase. By the time we reach the top, all three of us are huffing and puffing. At least the ladies have the excuse of being smokers. I just need to get off my backside and exercise more.

Standing there for a moment, catching our breath, we suddenly hear the sound of footsteps coming up the staircase. There are only two or three, then silence. We turn expectantly, wondering who's coming up. The answer is, nobody. The staircase is completely empty. I take a flashlight and go down again to make sure, confirming that nobody's there.

Perhaps, I think to myself, it could have been an echo of somebody walking around on the floor below? We quickly dismiss the idea. The footsteps were quite clearly on the steps themselves, and were loud and distinct enough to have been picked up on my voice recorder.

It seems than an invisible somebody is taking a definite interest in our little group.

"Are you coming up?" MJ asks, craning her neck to look down the staircase. Nobody answers. Nor is there anything out of place on the audio when we play it back. I'd been hoping for a possible EVP, but remind myself that I have no business feeling disappointed — after all, disembodied footsteps aren't something you get to experience every day.

Things take a turn for the strange when MJ begins to feel cold on her left-hand side, with pins and needles shooting down her arm. Lesley experiences the exact same sensation, but on her right side. Chills and pins and needles: an odd combination.

After a few minutes, they're both back to feeling normal again. Strange, though we can't definitively say it's paranormal. Nothing shows up on our voice recorders when we play them back, and none of our measuring equipment appears to be reading anything anomalous. I check my watch. It's getting on for two-thirty in the morning, and we're all getting tired. Determined that we're going to make the most of our last night here, there's no way we're stopping any time soon. More caffeine is in order.

Back in the break room, the team is getting a little boisterous, laughing and joking. It's probably due to the lack of sleep that plagues us all. Normally we're a little calmer and quieter than this, but I don't want to rain on anybody's parade so I decide to just keep my mouth shut.

After drinking what has to be my tenth cup of tea, I snag Wes and we go back down to the cellar. I'm interested to see what happens down there when it's just me and the professional jailor. We set up in the middle of the hallway and start our recorders running. It's still dark enough that the big prison guard is nothing more than a hulking shape to my eyes.

Wes runs the EVP session while I just hang back and observe. He's halfway between civilian Wes and full-on jailor Wes, speaking in a stern, authoritative tone but without being overtly confrontational. He starts by introducing himself again, establishing his credentials as a prison officer, and then tries to get any spirits that may be present to come forward.

As the session goes on, I find myself getting more and more annoyed at the sounds drifting down to us from the upper floors. The people in the break room are making so much noise that it sounds like a party is in full swing up there. The fact that they're showing absolutely no consideration for those of us who are on other floors (there's also a small group up on the second) is really starting to piss me off.

The more this goes on, the more I start to seethe. Just who the hell do they think they are, laughing and joking while there's work to be done?

As I write these words now, more than a year later, and relive the experience in my memory, it's very clear to me that my anger was growing out of all proportion to what was taking place above us. My mood was being affected by something external, of that I am completely sure — but I can only see that with the benefit of hindsight.

"It's so noisy," Wes whispers, as if reading my mind.

"A parade of headless bloody horsemen could come through here, and we'd never hear it," I respond bitterly. My resentment is beginning to show. Worse still, I don't really care who knows it.

Somebody whispers. It comes from the darkness behind Wes. I shine my flashlight beam over in that direction. Of course, there's nobody there.

"We might be getting somewhere," Wes says, cautiously optimistic. I hope so. With all of the hullaballoo upstairs, it's starting to feel as if we're wasting our time.

From somewhere up above us comes a loud cackle. I grit my teeth and try to stay focused. Wanting to have another crack at the unsavory male spirit we encountered earlier, Wes starts ratcheting up the intensity of his questioning, and while he's not actually provoking, there's a definite increase in the tension that's all around us.

"I may come from a different country, but I'm still a jailer," he declares. "Come forward and make yourself known right now."

Nothing.

"Don't hide in the shadows. Come forward and show yourself."

A loud growl splits the air. Unfortunately, it came from my stomach. Embarrassed, I mark it on the audio recording so we won't mistake it for anything paranormal later on. It's so loud, it actually echoes from the stone walls.

More noises drift down from the upper floors, contaminating any potential audio evidence we might capture. Angry at the lack of noise discipline, I swear under my breath, then have to mark that on the recording too. Far from getting productive results, it now feels as if we're just spinning our gears, and it's immensely frustrating.

After almost half an hour of attempted communication, Wes finally throws in the towel. Whoever it was that ran their fingertips through MJ's hair, they're not interested in interacting with us. It's hard not to see the entire session as having been nothing more than a colossal waste of time.

Then I remind myself that that's my anger talking. A good ninety percent of paranormal field research yields no results, which is why so many newcomers tend to drift away from it after their first few investigations. Unlike what you might see on TV, there's much more sitting around in the dark and far less ghostly activity than the editors of those shows would have you believe.

My foul mood is getting worse. Under normal circumstances, there's no way I would be getting this worked up over something like my team getting a little rowdy. Back in the break room, the whole group has assembled. As we munch our way through a few snacks, the sound of repeated knocking comes down from the ceiling at the far end of the room.

It's a dull thud, like a heel striking the floor. Lesley and Gaynor go upstairs to investigate, and confirm that there's nobody up there at all. Once again, they manage to localize the source of the knocks to the tea rooms, which are still locked up tight. Kirsten confirms that there's no way anybody could have gotten in there without having the keys.

Try as we might, we're unable to come up with a satisfactory explanation for the thuds.

"I get the feeling that they're being held back from talking to us," muses Wes, rubbing his chin thoughtfully. By *they*, I assume that he means the ghosts of Bodmin Jail. That begs the question of just who (or what) might be holding them back...and why.

It's hard to shake the feeling that he's right. The team splits up into smaller groups again and tries a few more experiments in different parts of the jail, but there's not a lot going on. I find myself wondering whether the light-hearted attitude taken by the team has placed a dampener on our last night at Bodmin. In terms of the professionalism we usually show, this hasn't exactly been our finest hour.

The more I think about it, the blacker my mood gets. By the time four o'clock rolls around, I'm stomping around the jail in a truly foul mood, one that's very out of character for me. Every once in a while, I catch Kirsten and some of the other investigators shooting me sidelong looks that seem to say, "What on Earth is *his* problem?"

It doesn't make a lot of sense to me either. Before tonight, Bodmin Jail had become my happy place, somewhere I eagerly looked forward to visiting and spending time investigating. Now, I can't wait to get out of here. For no apparent reason, I'm suddenly sweating, which is unusual for somebody inside an unheated stone building on a cold winter's night. A quick pulse check reveals that my heart is also racing, despite the fact that I haven't been physically exerting myself for at least the last hour. Just what the hell is going on with me?

Penny has to leave a few minutes early, so I walk her to her car. Not that she can't handle herself, but it's the right thing to do, just to be safe. She seems aware that my mood is off somehow, but she's polite enough not to ask me directly about it. My replies to her questions are terse and clipped. We say our awkward goodbyes, then I stand in the street and watch her drive away.

I walk back up the hill, brooding silently in the cold early morning air. As I pass through the main gates, the oppressive atmosphere hits me like a tsunami. In emotional terms, it's like being underwater. The team is wrapping things up, picking up their equipment and packing it away. Once everything is stowed, we haul it all outside into the front yard. People are milling around, making small talk. The only exception is Wes, who also looks less than happy for some reason.

The worst of the simmering rage is gone, but I'm still angry. The team assembles on the front steps of the jail for a group photo. I've got a face like thunder, glowering and sullen. For some strange reason, I feel distant and disengaged, as though I'm watching the proceedings from afar rather than experiencing them first hand.

After saying our goodbyes (unusually for me, I'm going with handshakes rather than hugs) the team begins to drift away one by one. Kirsten comes up to me and offers a smile. I do give her a hug, but it's stiff and awkwardly formal. "We'll see you again," she says. My response is non-committal and stony, the tone of voice like that of a spoiled child.

"Maybe. We'll see."

"Oh, you will." Kirsten is absolutely confident. "You'll be back. Just you wait."

I walk out through the main gate for what I'm sure is the very last time. After loading up the car, I turn and take one last look at the old place. Usually I'm elated at the end of a paranormal adventure, exhausted, over-caffeinated, and running on adrenaline. Not this time. I feel empty and divorced from reality in a way that even now, with the benefit of highlight, I find difficult to put into words.

I've offered to drive Wes back to his hotel. He's staying in a place a little closer to the Jail for the evening. There's little in the way of small talk between us on the short journey. There's a feeling of growing unease gnawing away at my gut, the unshakeable sense that something just isn't right. It's still dark when I drop Wes off, but dawn isn't all that far away.

It's been a real pleasure working with Wes, and I make a point of telling him that. He's gracious and polite, just as I have come to expect, but neither of us are acting quite like our usual happy-go-lucky selves. As I drive away, I don't bother to use the Sat-Nav. I know how to get back to Bolventor by now, which will take me straight to the Jamaica Inn, but something strange happens. I turn onto a roundabout, but don't take the Bolventor exit. Instead, I keep following it around until I've made a half-circle. Moving of its own volition, my hand hits the turn signal and I take the exit that will take me straightback into Bodmin.

I don't mean to imply that there was anything paranormal at work here. Most people drive on auto-pilot at the best of times; it's a terrible lack of awareness that costs far too many motorists their lives every year. When I was a student attending paramedic academy, for example, I was working full-time overnight and taking classes during the day, snatching a couple of hours of precious nap time in-between. I was so sleep-deprived that there were days when I literally could not remember anything about the drive home.

A similar sort of auto-pilot was at work now. I did not consciously intend to drive back to Bodmin, but nevertheless I somehow ended up on my way back there. The sense of unease I was feeling diminished with every mile I got closer to the jail. Something is forming in my mind, the idea that I had left the jail on bad terms and needed to make things right somehow. I didn't want to leave Cornwall, let alone the United Kingdom, without squaring things up with the spirits of Bodmin Jail.

The question was, would I make it in time?

CHAPTER SIXTEEN

Boom.

I turn right at the base of the hill, and there's the jail, just as I had left it a few minutes earlier. Or had it been a lifetime ago? My sense of time is completely shot, and it's something more than jet lag. The main gate is just being pulled closed by Kirsten. She looks up at me and I swear, she does not seem the slightest bit surprised to me.

Getting out of the car, I approach her sheepishly.

"See," she smiles. "I said you'd be back."

For the first time in hours, I smile too. "Yes, you did." I struggle to frame my words correctly, fighting my way through a mental fog. Kirsten isn't the least bit judgmental, and that mischievous twinkle is back in her eye.

"So, what brings you back?"

I explain that I don't feel right about the way the night ended up. My team and I were boisterous and rowdy, much more so than I felt was appropriate. I was worried that the spirits of the jail might misinterpret that as being disrespectful, something that none of us had intended. An apology was in order, coming directly from me to them. What does Kirsten think about that?

"I don't know. Why don't we go and ask them?"

It takes a good ten minutes for Kirsten to unlock the various and sundry doors that will let us back into the jail once more. She does it without the slightest complaint, working her way calmly and methodically from door to door. I'm already starting to feel better. My mind is growing less cloudy by the minute.

"You haven't been quite yourself once you came up from the execution pit," she remarks, turning one final key and swinging the last door open. "Neither has Wes. Neither of you have been quite right, but you were fine before you climbed down that ladder."

I ponder that for a moment as I follow her toward the staircase. I certainly hadn't felt like myself for the past few hours. It's fair to say that I have a bit of a temper when provoked, but the seething rage I had been feeling was far beyond normal. Did it really stem from having gone down into the hanging pit? Wes had been down there too, yet so had Stephen and other fellow investigators, and none of them were behaving abnormally.

Was it possible that Wes and I had been influenced by something that lurked in that part of the prison? Something malign that has been affecting our moods and behavior ever since we had climbed back up from the pit? It certainly wasn't beyond the realm of possibility. Now that I think back on it, I haven't been feeling like myself for at least the past few hours.

I follow Kirsten toward the staircase. The atmosphere seems charged to me, and it's hard to shake the feeling that we're being watched. Whether we truly are, or whether it's simply my imagination working overtime, I can't say for sure, but my money's on the former.

We take the steps down to the bottom level and walk from room to room, just taking it all in. Stand,ing in the most open spot that I can find, I clear my throat and feeling slightly embarrassed, start talking to thin air. I'm suddenly nervous.

"I'm really sorry for the way we all acted tonight. We were loud, we were boisterous, and at times we were unprofessional." My words are swallowed up by the shadows. Kirsten stands silently by, giving me the time and space to make my apology. Maybe my own eyes are playing tricks, but hers seem to be gleaming in the darkness. More than anything, I want to make it right between myself and the jail. "A lot of people lived inside these walls. Some served as jailers. Others served out sentences. Some of them never made it out alive. We didn't mean any disrespect, I promise you. It was just a case of...well, high spirits."

The pun is cringe-worthy, but I mean every word of what I've said. I just hope my true intent is coming across. Kirsten's silhouette gives me a little nod of what looks like approval.

"Good job," she says. "Now let's go upstairs."

I repeat the process on the ground level. By the time we reach the second floor, the first fingers of daylight are beginning to filter through the windows. The long central hallway is dim and grey. Things are already feeling much more peaceful than they have at any other point during the night. I should be exhausted, but my mind is completely clear again.

Kirsten and I are standing in the center of the corridor. I make the same apology as I have on the other floors, speaking in low, respectful tones. When I finish, it feels as if a great weight has been lifted from my shoulders.

BOOM.

I'll be the first to admit that I'm startled. The sound comes out of nowhere, loud enough to shake the hallway. I feel it reverberate through the soles of my shoes. Something very, very heavy must have fallen onto the floor at the end of hallway with great force — except there's nothing there. Thanks to the still-brightening daylight, I can see along the full length of the hallway very clearly. It's completely empty.

Kirsten and I exchange a look. I'm slack-jawed. She, on the other hand, does not seem to be the least bit surprised. "I think your apology has been accepted," she smiles. I smile back, convinced that she's right. Ever the skeptical investigator, I try to find a rational explanation, but nothing presents itself. For starters, we have complete visibility along the length of the corridor. The sound was loud, clear, and very distinct, sending a tremor through the floor beneath our feet. Kirsten and I both felt it, we both heard it, and more importantly, it was picked up by the digital voice recorder I'm holding. Unless somebody had broken into the jail without our knowing it (no mean feat), or had been hiding out in the building for the entire night and had now come out and had slammed the ceiling of the floor beneath us with something like a broom handle, then I had no way to rationalize what had just happened.

Frankly, any theory I could come up with seemed patently ridiculous. They also overlooked one all-important factor: the timing. I had just finished making a heartfelt apology to the spirits of Bodmin Jail when the phenomenon took place. Right down to my core, I feel that this was the jail's way of acknowledging that it accepted my apology, a sort of paranormal tip of the hat. Something along the lines of, "Alright sunshine, we'll let you off this time, but don't do it again."

Have you ever mended fences with somebody after having had a bad quarrel or feud? That's the closest thing I can compare it to. I no longer felt as if I had unfinished business here, that I would be leaving Bodmin on bad terms. The spirits and I were square again.

"You *knew* this was going to happen, didn't you?" I accuse Kirsten playfully as we make our way out to the main gate. She smiles impishly but refuses to give me a straight answer, preferring to let me figure it out for myself. (For the record, I still haven't). Crossing the courtyard, I pause for a moment, contemplating the execution block for what might be the last time. In the wan light of early morning, it looks even more sinister than it had the night before, though it seems hard to believe. There's a light breeze, and the noose sways gently from side to side. A sudden chill runs through me, and I find myself pondering just what it was that might have come back out of that pit with me earlier that night.

Could it have been some lingering remnant of one of the two prisoners who had been hanged there before executions stopped taking place at the jail, or perhaps more worryingly, might it have been something else entirely — a some*thing*, rather than a some*one?*

I may never know.

This time, the hug Kirsten and I share is one of warmth and friendship. Any lingering traces of anger and resentment are gone. The friendship extends not just to Kirsten but also to the jail itself, and I find myself hoping that someday, somehow, I will find myself walking back through the gates again, leading another team of paranormal investigators in an attempt to uncover more of Bodmin Jail's mysteries.

But for now, this is enough. More than enough. I feel privileged to have gotten one last burst of paranormal activity to send me off on my way. There's just one last thing to take care of before I bring one of the most intense investigations of my career to a close.

Closing my eyes, I imagine myself being engulfed in a bright white light. The light comes down from above in a column, enters through the crown of my head, and works its way from cell to cell in my body, washing any negativity away as it passes in a wave from top to bottom. This might sound ridiculous to some people, but I learned the hard way when I brought some kind of attachment home from a haunted location that engaging in some form of spiritual protection is of vital importance. Stephen had taught me this simple technique for staving off unwanted detritus, and now I closed out each investigation with it.

"Thank you, spirits of Bodmin Jail, for allowing me and my friends to spend time with you," I say, speaking slowly. "I am very grateful for the chance to interact with you...but now it is time for me to go home. No-one and nothing is permitted to attach itself to me, or follow me from here. You must stay here where you belong. This is your place, and here you are to remain."

I finish visualizing the light cleansing. Whether it literally works to protect me or not, I am unable to say for sure, but I can say with confidence that since I've started using this method, I haven't experienced any more unwanted paranormal phenomena at home, and I'd like that to remain the case.

The early-morning chorus of birdsong is in full swing, tweeting and chirping from the trees as the sun comes up. I take one last look at the jail through the open gate. Now that it's finally here, this moment feels bittersweet. Just two hours ago, I hadn't expected to come back here. Now I'm glad that I did. Bodmin Jail and those who inhabit it — both the living and the dead — have been good to my friends and I, and if the truth be told, I've grown rather fond of the place.

I get into my car and drive away, keeping one eye on the rearview mirror until the jail is out of sight. This time, unlike the last, I am finally content…and at peace.

Bodmin Jail has undergone some significant changes since my team and I left. The construction process kicked into high gear in the latter half of 2019, making it necessary for the jail to be closed to the public for several months. Thirty million pounds has been invested into turning the Naval Prison and the General Population Wing into a combination hotel and visitor center attraction which will, assuming all goes according to plan, allow thousands of new visitors to experience the jail for themselves. As part of the process, vital repairs to the crumbling structure are taking place, with much of the original layout being restored to something of its former glory.

It is well-known among members of the paranormal

research community that construction and demolition are very common triggers for increased activity at a haunted location. Unfortunately, as I write these words it is July of 2020, and the jail sits empty once more. The Covid-19 coronavirus is sweeping across the world, killing hundreds of thousands of people and forcing millions into a state of enforced social isolation. A national lockdown has been in effect since March, and both quarantines and social distancing measures seem likely to continue well into the foreseeable future.

Here on the other side of the Atlantic, riots are sweeping the country, a sign of the outrage people feel at the death of George Floyd at the hands of Minneapolis Police. Now that my working day is over and done with, I am sitting at home, putting the finishing touches to this book and thinking back fondly to my time at the jail. As I listen to the raw audio files once more, my mind goes right back to those nights in Cornwall. Once again, albeit just in my memories, I am climbing the staircases and exploring the cells of Bodmin Jail.

She — for some strange reason, I have come to think of the jail as a she — is waiting patiently, waiting for the living to return to her once more. Once this state of emergency is over, I sincerely hope that you, dear reader, will consider taking a trip to Bodmin and getting acquainted with the spirits of the jail for yourself.

Whatever else you do, please be respectful.

Richard Estep
Longmont, Colorado
July 14, 2020

Acknowledgments

Firstly, to you, the reader: Thank you for spending your hard-earned money and valuable time in order to read this book. It is my sincere hope that you have enjoyed it, and would ask you to please consider rating the book on Amazon's website. In the current writing market, books tend to live and die by their reviews and ratings, particularly on Amazon. Your help would therefore be greatly appreciated.

The author would like to extend his sincerest thanks to the following people, without whom this book would not have been possible.

First and foremost, I am indebted to those marvelous people, *Kirsten, Mark, Chris*, and *Vince*, along with the owner of Bodmin Jail, for their support, kindness, and willingness to help me tell the story of this grand old building.

Lesley, Wes, Gaynor, Caroline, Penny, and *MJ*, thank you for coming down to Cornwall and spending time with me, helping investigate the mysteries of Bodmin Jail.

Stephen and his partners, *Jill* and *Sharon,* for flying trans-Atlantic to do the same thing (bonus points to the crazy priest for doing it *twice!)*

My thanks are also due to all of the staff at Bodmin Jail, and also the good people at my favorite haunted inn, The Jamaica Inn, particularly *Sammy, Alan*, and *Karin.*

Tony Ferguson, for granting an interview and sharing his thoughts about the haunting.

Last, but by no means least, thanks to *Laura*, for looking over the manuscript and offering feedback, not to mention plenty of support along the way.

Much love to you all,
Richard

If you feel so inclined, please visit me over at my web page, **www.richardestep.net.** I love to hear from readers, so drop by and say hi!

Printed in Great Britain
by Amazon